THAT'S NOT MY CHILD

Five Generations on the Welfare Treadmill

Dr Frank Golding OAM holds degrees from Melbourne and London Universities. As an Honorary Research Fellow at Federation University Australia, he completed a PhD thesis on 'care' leavers and counter-narratives. His own experience in institutional 'care' underpins his advocacy and research on child welfare which has been published widely in journal articles, book chapters, and presentations in Australia and overseas. Frank has published more than a dozen books on a range of topics. He is a Life Member of CLAN, the peak advocacy body, and was awarded an Order of Australia Medal in 2018.

By Frank Golding—

An Orphan's Escape: Memories of a lost childhood

Body Corporate: a quick guide to the law in Victoria

Private Lives: Your guide to privacy law in Victoria

Common Ground: Your guide to body corporate law and living

Compendium of Good Practice: The role of schools in the vocational preparation of Australia's senior secondary students

Rural Law Handbook (with Tony Smith & Jan Bowen)

You and the Law: Children's rights and responsibilities (with Therese Fitzgerald)

Children and Laws around the World, Melbourne (with Therese Fitzgerald)

General Studies in the Open Classroom (with Doug Poad)

Refuge, Rescue and Reform: Voices of suffering and survival (with Dorothy Wickham forthcoming)

THAT'S NOT MY CHILD

Five Generations on the Welfare Treadmill

FRANK GOLDING

ARCADIA

First published 2024 by Arcadia
the general books' imprint of
Australian Scholarly Publishing Pty Ltd
7 Lt Lothian St North, North Melbourne, Victoria 3051

www.scholarly.com / enquiry@scholarly.info / 61 3 93296963

ISBN 978-1-923068-75-9

Cover design: Amelia Walker

Contents

PART 5 : LOST AND STRAYED

PART I
ORPHANS OF THE LIVING

If we are to learn anything from the great human resource of past experience, we have to begin by destabilising those self-congratulatory accounts of the past, because the past, like the present, is simply too complicated and too multiple to be told in any single story.

— Inga Clendinnen, 2006

History is not a single story. It is competing narratives, brought to life by different groups whose experiences are diverse and often challenge the dominant story a country seeks to tell itself.

— Larissa Behrendt, 2017

1

Remarkable things happen to unremarkable people

It is commonly agreed that family stories are most often passed on by mothers and grandmothers, but my mother and her mother revealed almost nothing to me about their lives and their family. It's clear to me now that they wanted to take some dark secrets to the grave. If truth is the ultimate right in a family, is secrecy the ultimate betrayal? Or does privacy trump everything? Story-telling, it is said, happens more frequently in families that are cohesive and close—families that talk a lot, and don't mind children asking questions. In these families, mothers and grandmothers chatter during family meals, holidays, birthday parties, long trips in the car. Key moments of disclosure over time create in the next generation a strong sense of the intergenerational self. A sense of the present embedded in the past, where you fit, who you belong to, who belongs to you (Duke, 2008). In families like mine, fragmented and dislocated, there is an abiding sense of unanswered questions about what happened to connect you to a past that lies within you.

Yet, anyone who knows where to look can find a surprising number of documents that record key events in the lives of even the most ordinary people. For a start, there are certificates of births, deaths and marriages although, as this book will show, the information in these official documents is not always accurate and can't be relied upon.

Sometimes remarkable things happen to unremarkable people. They enlist and fight in wars, get arrested and appear in courts, have affairs, get divorced, and have their dirty linen aired in the newspapers. Some carry the burden of cruel poverty and deprivation, are hit by calamities and fall into crisis. They then become the targets of oppressive interventions by government departments and public institutions. State surveillance creates unsuspected dossiers. You can find many facts about ordinary people buried in the archives. Not the whole truth, however—as we will soon see.

Even when written records are available in the archives, it is not easy to reconstruct a reliable historical narrative about ordinary people like the Sinnetts. Unlike the archived documents written by 'important' people, the facts about the Sinnetts were always written by public officials, clerks and other bureaucrats whose opinions and personal preferences often shape the written account. They hardly ever included the voice of the people they were controlling. The facts they recorded are selective, sometimes inconsistent, often inaccurate or misleading. Those who recorded the facts were not under oath, and were usually not accountable. It didn't much matter if the facts they recorded were convenient rather than precise. The truth can't be found simply by following the trail of written documents.

There are also frustrating gaps. While I was growing up in 'care', the Welfare recorded nothing at all about me or my family for long periods of time—as if our dark history required respite. Interpretation requires not only reasonable inference but also plausible leaps of imagination to fill the spaces and join the dots. While I want to tell the truth and nothing but the truth in this book, I can not claim to tell the whole truth because history can never be complete. There is always the possibility of another part of the story that was never told or never written down. Indeed, one of the key figures in the story told in this book—my grandfather, William Francis Salvador Sinnett—disappeared and, despite multiple searches by several experienced researchers, has not been found—yet.

While I was occupied in the frustrating search for my missing grandfather, a different story emerged piece by piece. It took the search to an unanticipated level and further back in time. A multi-generational story materialised that was messy, uncertain, and emotionally difficult at times. At some points, emotional distancing and empathy struggled for the upper hand. Sometimes I was tempted to make harsh judgments about my people. At times, I slid down the slope of blaming my mother and father for the mess we found ourselves in as children. Why couldn't they be our parents when we most needed them? Reading the records kept by the Welfare tempted me to assume our father was the villain of the piece. He was everywhere in the files. His alcoholic binges and public violence created an extended police history. In punishing him, the police and the Welfare punished us too, and our mother. Yet, she was hardly ever to be found in the Welfare records. Was I wrong to read her absence from the records, and her absenteeism in reality, as the shame of a neglectful mother?

Blame and shame are more complicated than that and I struggled with the tendency to see myself as a judge making findings about 'the facts'. To make meaning of a story that unfolded as chaotic and complicated, even unfathomable in places, required me to be part detective, part translator, part insider witness, part survivor. Yet, no matter how much I wiped my feet at the front door of this family history, I could not avoid leaving muddy footprints all over the floor.

This book raises the question whether the destructive fracturing of families like the Sinnetts might have been mitigated, if not avoided, had state intervention taken the form of support rather than punishment. Why are the failures of past policies and practices repeated? Why do we need to write these failures into their absence from government archives?

When the government of colonial Victoria introduced the *Neglected and Criminal Children Act* in 1864, it could hardly have expected it would have repercussions for the Sinnett family for five generations to come. In 1865, Edward Sinnett, aged 11, was the first of his family to be declared neglected (and later, criminal because he absconded from an Industrial School). Edward could hardly have imagined that, over the next century in successive generations, more than 30 children from his family, including the current author, would be incarcerated for the same 'offence' of neglect.

2

Questions in the night

My mother gave us up without a fight. That's what my father said. He told the Welfare she left us all alone in the house on that dark October night in 1940. What to believe? Dad told so many lies when he was three-bottles full. What could my mother do to stop Dad from hustling Bobby and me out of bed and whisking us away? She was thin and weak. He was strong and violent. He could take on any man. Including the police.

He left Billy alone. Five is old enough to stick up for your mum. I was just two and a half, and Bobbie was not yet four. Truth is: Billy was not his child. But if he wanted to punish our mother, he could have taken Billy too.

It's hard to remember the manic dark train ride to Melbourne, but I have read the files from the Boys' Depot at Royal Park—not that I trust them to be totally accurate. Dad planned to take us to the Depot, but it was closed for the night. Imagine our father struggling from one dim streetlight to the next with two heavy-eyed, grizzling kids, one on each arm, looking for somewhere to spend what was left of the night. The Salvation Army kept the lights on at the People's Palace in King Street. An oxymoron. An imperial palace for the down-and-outs of Melbourne and others desperate for a bed. In the morning, Dad took us from King Street to Royal Park. There the imperial march halted. The Receiving Depot in Royal Park was the first of the several warehouses for children where Bob and I were deposited for the long years of our childhoods. Billy would join us later on too.

It was a sunny August day in 1953 when I came home to my parents, in style. I spied them on the wharf at Station Pier in Melbourne waiting for the P&O liner *Strathnaver* to dock. I had been three months abroad. Eric Morton, the Superintendent of the Ballarat Orphanage, was there alongside them. They had fought one another for years. Now chatting happily enough. Clearing customs, I was ecstatic to learn then—and only then—that I was going home with my parents. Not back to the Orphanage. Twelve years late, but no longer an orphan of the living.

There was no manic train ride that day. A leisurely taxi to Ballarat and we were restored as a family in our newly rented, but very old, house in Main Road. The long voyage to the other side of the globe had brought an unanticipated close to my strange childhood. I think I carried two suitcases. One had basic clothes and a few souvenirs. The other carried the emotional baggage of an institutionalised childhood.

The scars were not so easily healed—for us and for my parents. They did what they could when we were all at home to rebuild our family. It was hard. We were toddlers when our mother lost us, and by the time we were finally 'released'—the Welfare used many words derived from the penal system—Bill and Bob had already been sent to work for a living.

At 15, I was on the tipping point between school and work, but my parents were clear about one thing. I should go on as far as I could with my schooling. I appreciated that clarity, having a goal like that was a novelty. I was elated by my unexpected escape from orphanage life. For the first time I could remember, I felt loved and wanted and could see a future. Yet I was confused by the continued presence of my past.

I was anxious and hesitant about how to behave. We were all lost. How would a 'normal' family behave? At times I resented my parents and silently blamed them for triggering my bizarre childhood. Above all, I was frustrated that they wouldn't discuss the past that damaged us all. I couldn't understand why they wouldn't explain why they abandoned us to the Welfare. *Did* they abandon us? Was it just our father, or did our mother give us up too? What was going on between them in the years we lived apart? Ask no questions, they said, and you'll be told no lies.

Every childhood lasts a lifetime. Unanswered questions don't just melt away in the mists of time. They lurk in the dark corners of shame and self-reproach. 'Normal' families, I discovered, celebrate milestones and revel in the cache of family archives—scrapbooks, letters and postcards, photographs, school reports, certificates, birthday cards. An array of memorabilia squirrelled away in shoeboxes, under beds, on top of wardrobes, in the spare room or the garage. I had nothing to show or tell about my baffling childhood. If you don't have a family history, you have to create one when people ask. At times I was reduced to making up a story, simply to get rid of the shame of the question—until the next time.

I was convinced that the true narrative of my childhood would remain a perplexity for the rest of my life. However, when I was in my 50s, a new door opened. Freedom of Information (FOI) laws were passed. Suddenly, personal dossiers and archived records that had been kept under lock and key all those years became accessible. I was told the archives had records about my strange past. Finally, upon application (and payment of the prescribed fee), I would learn the facts about my baffling childhood—or so I thought.

A large package of documents arrived in the post. I anticipated all manner of revelations about my parents, and about me too. But the Welfare took a surprising view of my entitlement. FOI seemed like FFI—Freedom from Information. They said I couldn't have my full record. They withheld pages, and purged whole paragraphs with whiteout fluid. I learned a new vocabulary. Documents 'redacted'; not to be 'released'; 'third party privacy'. What were these third parties doing in my file if they had not played a role in my childhood? The intruders turned out to be my parents, even sometimes my brothers Bob and Bill. I argued. How could parents and brothers be 'third parties'? They were my family. Information about my family was my personal information. I was entitled to know why I was made a ward of the state. What had my parents done to cause that to happen?

The very thought of the state holding a secret dossier with my name on it rankled. Why could a stranger in a government department read a file about me, but I could not? I was put back in my place. It was not my file. It was kept for administrative reasons. But no one in the administration could or would explain those reasons. The public servants thought me argumentative but I appealed their decision. And persisted. The Welfare 'released' a few more pages here, a paragraph there, a name somewhere else, a little more information about my father, almost nothing more about my mother. She had written only one letter to the Welfare. Five short paragraphs. I could have a copy but only after they had censored one of the paragraphs. I was perplexed—whatever did she reveal in that letter all those years ago that I was not allowed to see now? After more than a decade, knowing I would not give up, the Welfare relented and restored the redacted paragraph. Could I have struck gold? Fool's gold, sadly! It was about Billy who was sent to work on a farm, and wasn't being paid. Nothing we all didn't know already. That was one of the topics the family did discuss all those years ago.

After all those years, I think I've squeezed out all the information the Welfare has to offer. There are big gaps in what they recorded about my childhood, and what was included wasn't always reliable. Lots of questions remained unanswered. Did our father understand at the time that if he failed to pay the Welfare the agreed amount of maintenance for four consecutive weeks, we were automatically made wards of the state under the law? Did our mother know that? Did they know the Children's court would make us pay in the most painful way for his failure to pay in cash? Did our father attend the court hearing? Did he even know there was one? Did our mother know what was happening to her boys? Did anyone speak up for us—or for her? None of that is documented.

I wonder if anyone told our mother at the time—she never mentioned it—that the Receiving Depot in Royal Park gave Bob and me to a 'registered person' named Mrs Donoghue. A foster mother to replace our mother. Mrs Donoghue took us to her home in Northcote but, according to the file, she returned us to the Welfare after nine days. She wouldn't keep us, she said, because of our 'habits'. That's all that was recorded. Nothing more. What habits, at our age, could have caused her to reject us? She obviously didn't think it was her job to teach us better habits. Did she find other children more to her liking?

I was surprised to find a file note that said the Welfare

then sent Bob and me to the Andrew Kerr Memorial Home in Mornington. Like Mrs Donoghue, the Memorial Home remains a black hole in my memory. Hardly any documents survive from that short chapter in our story. Approaching Christmas in 1940. If they'd checked, they would have seen that it was Bob's fourth birthday that very day. The Home knew nothing about us. We were just like any other parcel delivery. The Matron countersigned the chauffeur's official delivery receipt. The chauffeur then handed her a certificate declaring that both of us were free from syphilis and epilepsy (but 'without blood tests'). That tiny scrap is the only trace of a medical history in my entire childhood. A few years ago, I found some small black-and-white photographs of the Andrew Kerr Home.

I ran a magnifying glass over them but I couldn't see Bob or me among the children playing on the front veranda, nor were we among the little soldiers marching double file along the avenue of pines. Where was our mother? Did she know we were in this Home? There's a strange connection to her father which I'll come to later in this story.

By April 1941 our parents must have resolved whatever it was that caused father's rage seven months earlier. They were back together. In the file, I found a letter our father wrote asking the Welfare to hand us back. In due course, his request was finally approved. I wonder what our mother made of the strict conditions they laid down. First things first, he was required to clear his debt to the Welfare and agree thereafter to maintain us 'without cost to the State'. Then he had to agree to any supervision by anyone the Welfare might appoint, and to tell them if he changed his address. He had to assure the Welfare that he would attend to any medical needs we might have. Finally, he was obliged to notify them if we ran away from home—or died. Like the syphilis and epilepsy certificate, this 'release on probation' document was not a written personal agreement, but a pro-forma fill-the-gap document. I presume every parent was given one when their children were being 'released'.

I guess our father didn't quibble, and once he signed the docket accepting all those stipulations, and paid the Welfare, he took delivery of us from Mornington—on three months' probation. Who was on probation—our parents or us with our habits? If all went well, the document said, we would be formally discharged to our mother in September. She must have been excited: her two little boys about to be handed back. But the language and tone in the dossier is as cold-hearted as the prison system.

That might have been the end of our bizarre childhood as orphans of the living. Childhood memory can be damaged by instability and insecurity. Why can I remember jumping from the top of a wardrobe into the safe arms of my laughing father? Was he drunk again, and jolly? Did he teach me how to leap out of our second-storey window, big brothers holding tight to the sheet as safety net? Giggling and cheering. No bones broken. Fragmented images of happy days. My third birthday with our parents at home.

Happiness is snatched away so cruelly. A second wild, reckless train ride to the Welfare in Melbourne. The official reported that Dad's hand was so shaky that she took the pen to complete the paperwork. The Welfare assigned us to another new foster mother, another 'registered person'. The file calls her Mrs Smith of Toorak—not an alias. Another mother, fleeting and unremembered. Weeks later, our parents were reconciled again. The Welfare gave Dad permission to pick us up from Mrs Smith and take us home once again. The dossier says we were 'on probation' again.

Many years later, my mother gave me a photo—a rare family shot. I calculate it was taken in July 1941 when Dad enlisted. He is in Army uniform. He stands behind his two boys. One hand is on Bob's shoulder and the other on our Mum, as if in proud possession. My hand rests in Mum's lap. Bill is more distant from his stepfather. Mum has one arm around Bill's shoulder. Her other arm is around my waist. She doesn't smile. Nor do we. Maybe the photographer's instruction. In a rare moment of candour in later life, but out of my earshot, Mum told my wife that she tore the photo in a rage then calmly patched it up with sticking plaster—Band-Aids. I inherited the original but had it restored. It's the only family photo to survive our fractured childhood.

Our third round with the Welfare came late the next year—this time in Ballarat. The Welfare, in its usual impassive prose, recorded that, 'Children were left in the C/O Mrs P Hills by their mother who has since deserted. It is believed that she has gone to Sydney.' Could that possibly be true? I've always thought it improbable that she deserted us. A document that was inexplicably found detached from the main files says she asked for us to be admitted to the Ballarat Orphanage because she was returning to her legal husband, Bill's father. It looks like her handwriting but she did not sign the document. I think it is more complicated than the paperwork suggests. In later life—at the time as well—I wish she had told us about what she was doing without us, in Sydney or elsewhere.

Determined to understand, I was able to trace Mrs Hills' daughter, Merrin, and her granddaughter Beverly, and they agreed to chat. She has memories of us all living together in Ballarat. It was a lively household: our mother and her three boys and Pearl Hills and her five children. (She would go on to have nine more children.) The Hills children called our mother Auntie Francie. According to Merrin, Pearl Hills told her stories that explain why our mother left. There was tension surrounding our mother's relationship with the two men in her life: Al Golding, the father of Bob and me, and her legal husband, Stanley Robinson, Bill's father. I will come to that problem in more detail later.

Merrin was eight at the time, old enough to have some insights. Merrin reckoned her mother thought she was the old woman who lived in a shoe, her capacity stretched to breaking point. With no sign that our mother was returning, one day Pearl Hills dressed us in our Sunday best, combed our hair, and marched us down to the police station.

I have only to hear the crunch of gravel underfoot to recall the policeman dragging the three of us—Billy too—towards that dark, forbidding Ballarat Orphanage where we would live for the next 11 years.

Our parents always insisted we couldn't talk about it, but there are things I wanted to tell them about the years I lost from my childhood. They were long years for me, filled with confusion, violence and fear. My place in the hierarchy of 200 other forsaken children depended on the bare-knuckle fights I won or lost. Once settled in, I found the days long and slow. The electric siren commanded us to wake up; do our jobs; line up for meals; march into school; march out of school; dodge the boss's long stick as he whacked stragglers on the back of their legs; do more jobs on the farm or the garden; guzzle a mug of warm tea and a slice of bread; join in another fist fight in the quadrangle; and so to bed with the deep fear that tonight I would be the one to be chosen after dark by the bad man or the big boy. The siren fractured my fears. Daylight brought relief, I had survived again. If I'd wet my bed, I had my nose rubbed in the sheets.

At breakfast I remembered the questions in the night. Was my mother sick and dying? Was my Dad away at the War? Why didn't they come and take me home? Why wouldn't anyone tell me? When would it end? Would it end? The deep fears of a little child stay with the adult forever. The lived experience lives on: the lack of love, the violence, the humiliation. Most of all the perpetual puzzlement about why it was the way it was.

3

Keepers of the secrets

I wish my mother had talked to me about her Sinnett family. She never answered my questions about my grandfather, her father. She said she didn't have any photos of him. For decades, the only thing I knew about her father was his splendid name, William Francis Salvador Sinnett. Was he Spanish? My father once said he was, but Mum shook her head. What was she hiding? He must have been a central figure in her sad life.

In unguarded moments, she did mention her sisters, softly dropping the names Minnie and Joyce into idle conversation. She hinted at other siblings, but whenever I asked about them, she clammed up.

One day, as if talking to some invisible ancestor, she uttered the phrase, the 'sins of the Sinnetts', then turned back to her crossword. Sins? From brief moments like that, I slowly came to perceive there was more to the pain of her life than the loss of her children to the Welfare in 1940. That loss was just one chapter in a much longer story. And all the while she was concealing an astonishing story about her own childhood, and her mother's life.

When I was an inmate of the Ballarat Orphanage, I knew more about Grandma Permella Sinnett than I knew about my mother. The Orphanage let us visit Grandma a few times a year after morning church. On each occasion, I went there thinking, perhaps she'd have a message from Mum. Imagine how we three boys hurried down Bakery Hill, pushed hard up hill on Dana Street, skirted the gaol via Armstrong Street, and rushed to Grandma's house in Skipton Street.

She never had any news for us. None she was willing to share. Grandma was the only link to my Mum. It puzzled me that Permella Sinnett was now Permella Marone. I wondered why she never talked about Bill Sinnett, her first husband and my mother's father. Secrecy, your name was Sinnett.

Decades later, I sometimes sit in my car outside the little weatherboard cottage at number 511 Skipton Street. Strangers own it now. Newly renovated—tarted up with a bold green frontage and bright red terracotta pots. The high fence can't obstruct my images of childhood. I could feel Permella's physical presence imprinted deep in my memory of that house. Down the dark side passageway to the lean-to kitchen at the rear, I see Grandma and her second husband, old Jack Marone, and their two children, Jacky and Catherine. Permella's sister—our Auntie Lizzie—and her husband, Uncle Bill Bennetts, are there too. In my child's eye, Grandma is grey and stooped, but when I calculate the years, I realise she was perhaps 50 at most when we first knocked at her door.

Grandma stoops down to the wood oven to take out the mutton sizzling in fat. She turns the spuds and onions and bastes the lot. My nostrils send a surge of hunger to my tummy. Auntie Lizzie puts in the parsnips and carrots. 'Another 30 minutes and Bob's your uncle.' 'Who's making the gravy?' 'Where's the flour?' The men open another bottle of Ballarat Bitter for themselves, and pour stout and lemonade for the ladies. Jacky pours sarsaparilla cordial for us young ones. Uncle Bill Bennetts sets up the fold-up stools and some logs cut to size and we all squeeze around the rickety table, some eating off our knees. Second helpings if we want, and accustomed as we are to gobbling and guzzling at the Orphanage, we certainly do. Marvelling at our appetites, Grandma puts another loaf of bread on the table cutting it in chunks so we can mop up the gravy. Then the plates are whisked away for washing up.

Full of food, but hungry for information, we linger, waiting for any crumbs of news that might fall off the edge of the chitchat. Auntie Lizzie passes around a tin of State Express Ready Rubbed and papers, and they take turns to roll thin smokes. Young Jack always puts his behind his ear for later. The grown-ups chat, as if indifferent to our presence. Yet their conversation is guarded against young ears cocked for the tiniest scrap that might clarify our odd position as inmates of an orphanage. We are not orphans; they know that. Grandma would know how desperate we are for news of our Mum, but never a word did she speak to give us hope.

When Jacky lights the gas lamp in the kitchen, it's time for us to go home. Back to the Home. On a good day, the household can scrape together a few pennies for our tram fare. If we run hard along the Yarrawee Creek through White Flat and the shallow channel that run through the back of the Orphanage, we can still be home before dark and save the pennies to spend on a bag of broken biscuits the next day.

Reality returns in my cold, iron bed at the Orphanage. Nothing gained. No news about Mum. No messages from her. None the wiser about the paradox of being an orphan of the living.

Bill Sinnett, my grandfather, has always been a mystery. I never met him. Over the years, I formed the view that he was at the heart of the family narrative, and I determined to reconstruct his life as best I could from whatever other sources I could find outside the family. His birth certificate showed he was born in Melbourne in 1894, so he and the intimate witnesses to his life were long dead. To my surprise, readers of my memoir *An Orphan's Escape* provided information that opened pathways. One, a previously unknown cousin, even supplied a photograph of a young Billy Sinnett. Did my mother have a copy? As she grew older, she said she had a few photos but was ever reluctant to get out the dusty box from the back of her wardrobe. In the photo supplied by my cousin I see a handsome dandy, but I like his deep brown eyes and smooth strong jaw.

The National Archives of Australia initially said there was no record of a Bill Sinnett as an enlisted man, but months later I asked them again. This time they found a detailed military dossier from World War 1. Some facts began to emerge from that file. When he sailed overseas, my mother was not yet born. By the time he returned she had had her third birthday. The significance of that space in time did not sink in to me at first glance.

I was proud to find that my grandfather fought in the 'Great War'—at Gallipoli and Pozières, no less, sites of Australian folklore. I was thrilled to find another photograph of him in the archives at the Australian War Memorial. Given its origin, I would be surprised if my mother ever saw this one. It was a formal shot of part of his 22nd Battalion taken at Franvillers on 30 May 1918 towards the tail end of the War. The line-up showed 80 soldiers of all ranks, yet somehow my eye went straight to my grandfather. He was centre front, sitting next to the battalion mascot, Bill the goat. I prefer to think my eye went directly to him because of some more mystical reason.

Following these leads, I found a version of my grandfather and his friends in a number of military service files, in official reports and a swag of published personal diaries and letters. None of them his, but all relevant to understanding his life in the army. His unit had kept a daily diary.

I decided to follow his trail literally on the old battle sites. I wish my mother could have come with me. I think it would have been an eye-opener for her as much as for me. In Turkey, I hiked over the ridges of Gallipoli and wondered how he clambered up the difficult hills into the face of Turkish machine guns. Later, I travelled around the Western Front in a borrowed Peugeot and imagined running beside him in no-man's-land on the Somme. At Pozières, I envisaged him being pulled out of the trench where he had been buried alive and stretchered out with his chest riddled with shrapnel. In green and pleasant Hampshire, I pictured his recuperation in the military hospital (once state-of-the-art but now abandoned and derelict), eager to return to the fray to share the triumph in the tailwind of 1918. I conceived a loving meeting in 1919 when he and Permella, his bride, were reunited and my mother, their child, would see her dada for the first time.

I fancied my grandfather a hero. That's what I wanted him to be; but I found a man far less heroic. More battlefields opened up at home after the war. There were times I wanted to shut the annals and put him back on the shelves. In the maze of coroners' reports, police records, dossiers held by welfare agencies and courts, and contemporary newspapers, I began to see why my mother and her mother held their tongues. Muddy footprints led to a family at war with itself and with the Welfare.

The more I learned about the men in the lives of my mother and grandmother—husbands and other partners too—the more I came to understand how much there was to know about these two women, and the ways men colonised their lives. In different ways, my mother and grandmother were the real custodians of a much more complex story than I ever anticipated.

In 1972, I moved with my wife and children to a new job in South Australia. I was preoccupied with building a house, managing new colleagues, and making new friends, but my parents and I kept in touch intermittently. They visited us later that year, and my Mum casually mentioned that her mother had died in July that year. I was surprised she hadn't bothered to call us or send a telegram about the sad news. I was even more surprised when she said that she didn't go to her mother's funeral. How could she be so nonchalant? It didn't occur to me to dig any deeper at the time because Grandma Permella Sinnett was 75 years old and hadn't been in good health. Mum didn't put me right when I assumed her mother had died peacefully in her sleep. I think she knew the terrible truth but kept it to herself.

I find the documentary aftermath distressing, mainly for the description of her death (which I will write about later) but also for the inaccuracies, whether careless or calculated. The death certificate issued by the coroner lists the two children from her second marriage, John and Catherine Marone, but my mother was the only child mentioned from her first marriage. By now I knew that Permella had four other children, but why were they omitted from the death certificate? The Ballarat *Courier*'s notice of Permella's death created further confusion. It read in full: 'MARONE, Permella: beloved wife of the late John, loving mother of Jack, Catherine (Mrs Singh), loved grandmother of Mark. (24/7/1972).' My mother was on her death certificate, but she was excluded from the public notice. And so were we, her Golding grandchildren—and there were her other grandchildren too. I wondered if my mother knew why these discrepancies happened. I wish now that I had asked my mother for answers.

Did my mother ever visit the Ballarat New Cemetery to see her mother's grave? If she did, was she surprised to find her mother shared the grave with Catherine Adams, Permella's mother, and her first son, Frank Sinnett, my mother's baby brother who had died more than 40 years earlier. It's perplexing: Permella is buried with her young son, but young Frank is not included on her death certificate. There was no logic to it at all.

I suspect that my mother did not know about another significant grave in the Ballarat Cemetery, not more than 100 metres away from the grave shared by her mother, grandmother and brother. The neglected weathered headstone askew among the weeds simply tells the world it was a plot for the 'Ballarat and District Orphanage 1865'. No other dedication. No names for the 26 children who died in the Orphanage. Placed in 'care' as neglected children, they were neglected in death. The Cemetery records the names of the children buried in this mass grave. Would my mother be surprised that her sister, Joyce Sinnett, was one of the neglected children? Joyce was aged 12 when she died. I might be wrong, but I suspect my mother knew nothing about the sad life her sister Joyce lived in the Orphanage after she was forcibly separated from her family. This is another story to tell—but later.

Only a short walk from Joyce Sinnett and her mass grave

there is another mass grave—even larger than the Orphanage gravesite. You have to know what you are looking for to find the unmarked grave for anonymous paupers—poor souls apparently with no family willing to pay for a decent burial. This is the last resting place of old Jack Marone—Permella's second husband, my mother's stepfather. Old Jack Marone and Joyce Sinnett have this in common: they were both separated from their families and died while in the 'care' of an institution. There is more to tell about that later too.

Whatever caused so much family fragmentation in those troubled years had not been resolved even by 2004 when my mother's half-brother John Marone died, a bachelor aged 77. Again, the notice in the local paper mentioned only an abridged family. Jacky—as I knew him—was described simply as 'the loving brother of Catherine Singh and Uncle of Mark'. No mother or father, no other siblings, no other nieces and nephews (there were many).

I was determined to attend Jacky's funeral. Catherine and Mark were surprised to see me. They were the only ones in attendance—apart from a celebrant and a cemetery worker. Catherine and Mark had chosen to bury Jacky in another section of the cemetery distant from the separate graves of his mother and father. A family fragmented in death, as in life.

When we shared a pot of tea and a Milk Arrowroot biscuit back at the house afterwards—the site not only of Jacky's death but also Permella's tragedy—I tried to steer the conversation towards the questions that perplexed me. We had never been close, but we had once been familiar; but now Catherine responded to my conversation-starters on family history as if I were an unwanted intruder. After a decent period, I approached Catherine again as sensitively as

I knew how, but again she did not respond to my questions. When I returned to the cemetery months later, I found Jacky's headstone in place. It repeated the limited declaration: 'the loving brother of Catherine Singh and Uncle of Mark'. What brought them to exclude the rest of their family—my mother's family, my family?

Catherine often came to our house in Main Road for meals with her husband Jimmy Singh—James Sothera Singh. My mother laughed about her being 'always pregnant'. She certainly had many other children besides Mark. When James Sothera Singh died in 1969, his death certificate listed eight children—but it was a shock to see that Mark was not listed as one of them. When Catherine died in June 2010 aged 81, her death certificate listed nine children, but only six of them were named in the local paper at the time (*Courier* 19 June 2010: 13). Mark provided the information for that certificate, and when he swore an affidavit for probate following Catherine's death, he named all of her nine children (VPRS 17379, P0003, Unit 381). Who or what were they trying to conceal? If anything? It's too late to ask now. Mark died in November 2015 aged just 48. I wonder how much he would, or could, have unravelled of the strands of our tangled family.

The manipulation of the records of bereavements both intrigues and disconcerts me, but perhaps it's a distraction from the real story. It's my mother's father I've really been searching for, Bill Sinnett, the grandfather I never met. I can't find a grave in the Ballarat cemetery or anywhere else in Australia or overseas for my grandfather. His final destination remains a mystery. His name was never spoken in our house or in Permella's house on our visits. That mystery drove me to go back to a time before he was even born—and to further mysteries.

The Andrew Kerr Memorial Home, Mornington Victoria. I have no memories of living there, but Bob and I are documented as inmates from Christmas 1940 to April 1941 (Photos: Anglicare Victoria).

Mum had the only photo of the family taken about 1941.

The Ballarat Orphanage at the end of the tramline in Victoria Street, our residence from early 1943 until mid-1953 (Photo: Ballarat CAFS).

Part of the 22nd Battalion at Franvillers on 30 May 1918. Grandfather Bill Sinnett (enlarged at right) sits with the Battalion mascot also called Bill (Photo: National Archives Australia).

Bill Sinnett, my mother's father, the grandfather I never met (Photo: Lorraine).

The *Sir Harry Smith*, a training ship and 'a receptacle for young boys from the industrial schools': *The Australian News for Home Readers*, 20 April 1867 (State Library of Victoria).

In 1867, The Nelson was handed down to the Colony of Victoria to become a training ship and reformatory for wayward boys (State Library of Victoria).

The village of Pozières before the War (above) was transformed during the fierce battle (below), a testament to the lunacy of war (Photos: Australian War Memorial).

Above: the common grave of 26 children from the Ballarat Orphanage at the Ballarat New Cemetery. *Below*: the names and ages of the children were finally acknowledged on a plaque in 2008 with the headline 'Ballarat Orphanage Interments' (Photos by the author).

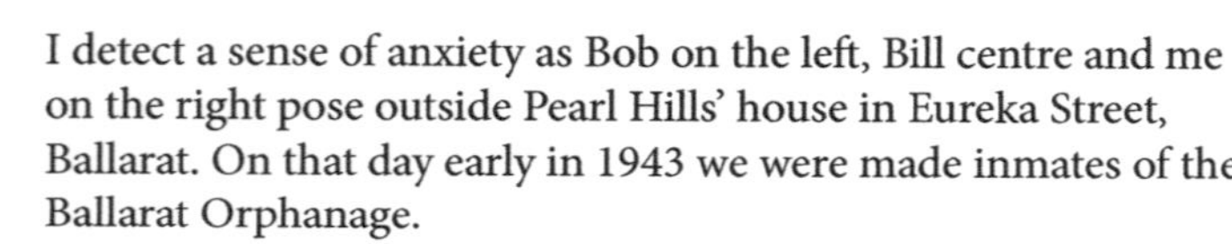

I detect a sense of anxiety as Bob on the left, Bill centre and me on the right pose outside Pearl Hills' house in Eureka Street, Ballarat. On that day early in 1943 we were made inmates of the Ballarat Orphanage.

Outside the Orphanage in around 1950. I am on the left, Bill centre and Bob on the right. Obviously, our parents had visited for the day. It was rare for institutionalised children to have personal gifts or toys, and even more uncommon to have childhood photographs. These photos have been in the possession of our Aunt Minnie for decades before cousin Lorraine passed them on.

PART 2
DARK SHADOWS OF YOUTHFUL DEPRAVITY

A neglect of this duty [to support the newly opened Melbourne Orphan Asylum] will entail upon you, not only morally, but politically and socially, serious responsibilities. Remember that these orphans, if not carefully looked after, will shortly go upon the town and become pickpockets. Of the prospects of the female portion, I need say nothing: I leave that to your own understandings. If this be the case, do you not think that you are bound by every means in your power to take care that this evil does not fall upon society?

— Governor Sir Charles Hotham, 1855

4

Youthful vagrants: neglected or criminal?

Bill Sinnett's father, Edward John Sinnett, came to Australia, as hundreds of thousands did, in pursuit of the golden dream of making their fortune on the goldfields in Ballarat, Bendigo, Castlemaine. Edward abandoned his dream when he met Eliza Morrison in Geelong the common port of arrival. They married at Christ Church Geelong seven weeks after first meeting, by which time she was known as Eliza Halse (#540/23838). The real name of Eliza Morrison/Halse remains a mystery. Just prior to sailing to Australia on the *Victory* in 1852, Eliza Halse was christened in London. She was 21. Her parents were listed as Joseph Halse (a baker) and Elizabeth Bronker, residents of London. For reasons unknown, Eliza travelled to Australia under the name Eliza Morrison (VPRS 14). Yet as soon as she put foot on Australian soil—on Christmas Eve in 1852—she became Eliza Halse again. Decades later, the maiden name Morrison emerged again. She must have shared it with a small number of insiders because it appeared on the marriage certificate of her son in 1879 and finally on her own death certificate in 1918. In both cases, the recorded information was supplied by those close to her in the Sinnett family. Can we ever know what secrets Eliza Halse/Morrison/Sinnett was hiding?

With men rushing to the goldfields creating a shortage of labour, Edward had been snapped up as a drayman at Pettavel's vineyard in the picturesque hills of Germantown (renamed Grovedale in 1915). The position came with the bonus of on-site accommodation for his wife and infant child, also Edward John. It did not take long for the wine maker, Mr Barbier, to find that Edward was 'much given to drink'. Too much so. Despite the acute shortage of labour, in October 1855 Barbier gave him the sack. Edward was distraught. With a wife and young child to support and dependent on his employer for both wages and accommodation, he set out to beg for another chance. In the haze of the late afternoon sun, however, he stopped for a pick-me-up at Fitzgibbons Public House. Suitably fortified, and carrying a bottle of rum as reinforcement, he resumed his journey to regain his job. Edward's condition failed to impress. Angry by not being rehired, Edward finished what remained of the rum and hitched a ride home on the back of Julien Grellet's bullock dray to convey the bad news. When they arrived, the bullocky told Eliza that Edward was dead drunk. In fact, he was just dead. 'Died by the visitation of God in a natural way,' the coroner's jury concluded, 'hastened by the excessive use of ardent spirits' (VPRS 24/P; Geelong *Advertiser and Intelligencer* 16/10/1855: 2).

Eliza Sinnett was just 24 and had no means of support in a colony that offered little for single mothers and their children. She needed to find a man much in need of a wife. Despite her enigmatic past, Eliza soon found a new husband in Geelong. Richard Jesse Stokes, a butcher of Buninyong near Ballarat, was a bachelor some 20 years her senior. Young Edward Sinnett became Edward Stokes after his mother married Stokes at St Paul's Geelong on 12 February 1857.

Eliza and Edward did not find life under Stokes much to their liking. The local newspapers tell a sorry story of physical and emotional abuse. On 17 October 1861, when Edward was eight years old, the *Advertiser* reported that Stokes, then in a labouring job at Lethbridge, was summoned to appear at the

Central Police Court at Geelong for assaulting his stepson. Edward had run away from home on several occasions because, he told the police, Stokes had whipped him. He showed police the marks on his body 'in proof of ill-usage'. The police cared for him for several days—in a cell, I suspect, for there were no other public facilities in the area. At his trial, Stokes denied he'd ever beaten him so severely as young Edward made out. He told the court that Edward was 'a badly disposed child'. Furthermore, although he was under all but constant surveillance, 'he managed to get away from home from time to time, and enter people's tents, helping himself to money or anything else that came within his reach. He also had a strong disposition to set the neighbours' tents on fire.' The Magistrate questioned Edward's mother. She was reluctant at first but after some hesitation, she confessed that Stokes frequently beat her son. The magistrate asked whether Stokes ever ill-used her, to which she replied, 'not very often, Sir'.

Stokes was clearly a brutal bully, but the magistrate was not moved to penalise Stokes beyond issuing a caution about his future behaviour towards Edward. He did not issue to Stokes a similar warning about beating his wife. Stokes strolled home a free man with his wife and stepson two paces behind, rightly fearful that the magistrate's advice would not be heeded.

Six months later, Stokes placed an advertisement in the local newspaper repeated over a number of days. He was offering a reward of £1 for information concerning the whereabouts of his runaway stepson (Geelong *Advertiser* 3/3/1862).

Stokes's advertisement was placed directly under another one offering **£10** for two missing horses. Everything is relative!

The local paper confirmed that Stokes was not concerned for Edward's welfare. It reported that a William Hazill had come before the court 'to claim sundry monies expended in boarding and educating a boy named Stokes under the following circumstances' —

> *THE BOY STOKES AGAIN—The child in question, a reward for whose discovery has been for some time advertised in this paper, has become notorious for running away from his home at Lethbridge, where his stepfather it has been alleged, at the Police Court here over and over again, cruelly ill treats him, various marks on his body testifying to the rough usage he has experienced. On the 11th January last an arrangement was entered into by the stepfather with the plaintiff [Hazill], by which the latter was to take and adopt him as his own son, receiving from Stokes 6s per week as an equivalent.*
>
> *Hazell [sic] appears to have performed his part faithfully, for the boy appeared in Court very decently attired, and the man assured the Bench he sent him constantly to school. Latterly it appears Stokes, the stepfather, has purchased some cows and now insists upon the boy being returned to him that he may employ him as a cowherd, which request Hazell positively refuses to comply with. He now stated that he was willing to abandon all claim for payment provided the bench would guarantee him possession of the child, who would only run away again, he stated, if returned to the questionable care of the stepfather. The bench appeared desirous to have the man Stokes before them, and for this purpose adjourned the case for a fortnight* (*Advertiser* 12/4/1862: 3).

Despite the evidence submitted in these proceedings, Edward found himself back with Stokes again where his mother, herself a continuing casualty of his brutality, could offer no protection. Stokes obviously also exercised his conjugal rights—by now Eliza had her hands full with four new children (and three more would follow).

When the family shifted to Ballarat, Edward again absconded and lived off his wits among the growing band of 'urchins, waifs and strays, street Arabs and youthful Bedouins' (Ballarat *Star* 7/2/1860: 3). Voicing the fears of genteel folk, the *Star* and local magistrates had been leading a campaign to rid the streets of these rascals. Children like Edward must be rescued from 'the dark shadows of youthful depravity or destitution' and trained to be god-fearing and industrious (*Star* 5/12/1859: 2).

It was only a matter of time before Edward was caught committing what the paper called an 'instance of juvenile depravity'. In February 1864, he stole a silver watch and chain. Standing in the dock, he looked so young that although he was now ten, the reporter assessed him to be about seven or eight. Edward told the court his father was dead and he did not live with his mother. The owner of the stolen goods, Mrs Hobley, shed a tear and withdrew the charge. The police, however, returned Edward to his mother and stepfather with a stern warning to mend his ways (*Star* 24/2/1864: 2, 4). They did not ask Edward why he was absconding nor did they, this time, warn Stokes to mend his ways.

A year later, there was no compassionate Mrs Hobley to save Edward when he was brought before the Ballarat magistrates again (now correctly described as aged 11). This time, he was charged with a different kind of offence. The *Star* (28/1/1865: 4) reported:

> *A YOUTHFUL VAGRANT—A little boy named Edward Synnett* [sic] *was charged by his mother with vagrancy. She stated that her husband was willing to contribute towards the boy's support in the Reformatory. The case was remanded until Monday, in order that the father might have an opportunity of appearing to enter into the necessary recognizance for payment.*

Three days later (31/1/1865: 4), the *Star* amended its report:

> VAGRANCY—John Edward Synnett, a little boy about eleven years of age, was charged by his stepfather with vagrancy. The case was remanded for a week, in order that it might be ascertained what amount would be charged for his maintenance in the Reformatory.

Had the stepfather bullied Eliza to rid him of her 'depraved' child? Or did Eliza mean only to frighten Edward into mending his ways? Did she have second thoughts about charging her little boy when she discovered that, under the new *Neglected and Criminal Children's Act* 1864, he faced a sentence of not less than a year and up to seven years imprisonment? Three days before he was due to appear in court, she took Edward to the Holy Trinity Anglican Church in Buninyong and had him christened. Did she hope to sway the magistrates with an act of contrition? If so, the magistrates were not impressed. Sinnett, the sinner, must be punished. They sentenced him to four years in the Melbourne Industrial School. His stepfather was ordered to pay 3/6d a month for maintenance.

The *Star* was not strict with the truth. It referred to Stokes as Edward's father-in-law (7/2/1865: 4), and strictly speaking, Edward was not charged with the crime of vagrancy—as the newspaper had it—but with its juvenile equivalent, being a neglected child. Under the new law, any child could be sent to the Industrial School if the parents declared they were unable to control them and agreed to pay money for maintenance.

I digress, but I am reminded of my mad train rides three-quarters of a century later when my father too would put his children into the hands of the Welfare on the understanding that he would pay maintenance to the Welfare. The process had not changed after all those decades. We the children were charged with being neglected—not the parents. When our father reneged on his maintenance payment, the system punished his neglected children—and again, did nothing about his neglect as a parent.

Edward was sent to the Melbourne Industrial School then situated in the Immigrants Home near Princes Bridge on the Yarra River. Only months later, the Ballarat Orphan Asylum opened its doors for the first time, and in the years to come, children in our family would come to know that institution so well. This local orphanage would have been a better option for Edward, but he might not have been acceptable to the orphanage governors. Having close regard to 'legitimacy, morals or respectability', they would accept only 'the Orphans of honorable parents'. While they applauded the police in their fierce determination to rid the streets of offending or offensive children, their orphanage would not become 'a receptacle for the criminal and abandoned' (Ballarat Orphan Asylum 1866: 12).

In 1865, Edward was the 707th of 868 children—three-quarters of them under the age of ten—rounded up by the police and incarcerated in makeshift accommodation, including the Melbourne Industrial School (*Annual Report* 1867: 3-5; and *Argus* 13/7/1867: 6). I know my great-grandfather was the 707th because the children were all given a registration number in order of admission—and the sequence continued up to 1962. In 1940 Bob and I became numbers 66851 and 66852 while Bill, committed later, was 68479 (VPRS 4527). Inside the walls of many institutions, children were stripped of their name and personal identity and were addressed by another allocated number for daily life (Senate 2004: 92-94).

Adult survivors who were incarcerated as children are

notoriously reluctant to talk about their life inside—some never tell even their nearest and dearest in later life (Senate 2004: ch. 6). My great-grandfather Edward certainly learned to keep his thoughts and feelings about his childhood to himself. However, there is a surprising amount of documentary evidence, some of it general and some of it specific to Edward, a little of it first-hand, enough for me to give a plausible account of the five years he spent locked up in various institutions.

5

Prisoner 707

Prisoner number 707 was 11 years of age when he arrived at the Melbourne Industrial School at Princes Bridge on St Kilda Road on 18 February 1865. Edward Sinnett found standing room only. The police were rounding up more children every day although the facility was dangerously over-crowded, lice-infested and disease-ridden. An outbreak of ophthalmia was leaving many children completely blind and, in all, 117 children would die that year (*Annual Report* 1867: 3). Edward might have been safer on the streets of Ballarat than in protective custody of the standard provided at the makeshift Industrial School.

Children were moved from the Princes Bridge facility as soon as sleeping quarters were completed at a new Industrial School under construction at Sunbury, a rural town north of Melbourne (*Argus* 30/10/1865: 5). Edward's lot would not improve when he was transferred to Sunbury. The place was a shambles: not only were the buildings incomplete, the food was rancid, sanitation was primitive, and sick children shared unheated, overcrowded dormitories with the rest of the inmates. Ophthalmia was soon raging there, too (Musgrove 2024).

On his first night at Sunbury, Edward found himself locked in a dormitory with some 80 other boys. Handed a straw mattress, a blanket, two sheets, a coverlet, and two rough pillows, he was hard pressed to find a space to bed down. All 80 boys shared three chamber pots through the night until they were released into the exercise area at dawn. Thereupon, they washed in a single tub of water sharing two makeshift towels and a single comb (Brogden 2000: 29, 31; Musgrove 2024). Order was kept through punishment so excessive that it would become the subject of a formal inquiry along with allegations of 'improper practices between boys and girls', and rumours that some male staff engaged in 'improper relations with girls' (Melbourne *Argus* 1/12/1865: 5).

When Edward turned 15, he would be allowed to return to his mother, the same age as I was when I was returned to my mother four generations later. That was the plan, but it soon went awry. Edward met up with his friend Isaac Brailsford (aka Beresford) in the Industrial School. They had been pals when making what they could of life on the streets of Ballarat. When Isaac was picked up by the police, he was also 11 years old, and already world-weary through a childhood of grief and pain. When Isaac was still an infant, the Ballarat police had prosecuted his father, William Brailsford, for repeated assaults on his wife. They described him as 'an indecent brutal fellow' (Ballarat *Star* 21/1/1860: 4). As soon as he was released from gaol, Brailsford skipped town and was never seen again.

Then at aged 6, Isaac had seen both his mother, Margaret, and his older sister, Amelia then just 9 years old, sent to prison for petty theft—in the same prison but separate cells. A year after their release from gaol, Amelia was called to give evidence at her mother's inquest. Her death was attributed to 'apoplexy due to very intemperate habits' (VPRS 24/P000, 1861/274). Amelia was in no position to look after her little brother.

In June 1864, three years after his mother died, the police arrested Isaac in Ballarat for stealing six ducks. He was just four feet two inches tall at the time and had to stand on tiptoes to tell the magistrates his mother was dead and he didn't know the whereabouts of his father. They sentenced him to six months' imprisonment—one month for each duck. The authorities could hardly imprison such a young boy. And what was to become of him after the six months sentence had been served? Sunbury was, apparently, the only solution.

In the bedlam that was Sunbury, Isaac and Edward Sinnett were becoming what they were both locked up for—a neglected child. They decided together not to put up with the appalling conditions at Sunbury. Within a month, they were over the wall, and out. The *Victoria Police Gazette* (*VPG*) reported that the escapees were wearing distinctive 'padlocked striped jumpers' before their escape, but they had broken into the clothing store and taken off in disguise (*VPG* 16/3/1865: 127). That ploy didn't work for long. In the next issue of the *VPG*, the police announced their recapture. They nabbed Edward at Batesford, a village near Geelong where his real father had lived (VPG 30/3/1865: 143).

The friends were now separated: Isaac aboard the hulk, *Deborah*, Edward back to Sunbury. Having crossed the thin line between 'neglected' and 'criminal,' Edward was soundly thrashed and put to hard labour. In June, he was transferred to the brig *Sir Harry Smith*, a floating Industrial School moored off Sandridge (VPRS 11976).

On the prison ship, the barber shaved Edward's head, inspected him for lice, and supervised his bath. The quartermaster issued him with a hammock, sleeping gear, and uniform. The ship's tailor supplied needles and thread and taught him how to mend seams and sew on buttons and patches. The captain, flanked by the ship's police, recited the rules for newcomers. Obey all orders. No quarrelling, no fighting, no abusive language. Maintain the strictest silence during duties. Report 'skulkers and lazy characters'. Detect thieves on board. Abstain from buying or exchanging clothes.

By 8 o'clock that night, Edward lay exhausted in his new hammock, but whatever sleep he managed was terminated abruptly by the 5 a.m. bugle. A jab in the ribs alerted him that he had 15 minutes to prepare his hammock and possessions for inspection. Satan found no idle hands on this industrious ship. He was assigned to scrub the decks, lower the boats, and wash them out before cleaning himself up for breakfast at 6.30. Half an hour later, he was hard at it again until 9.00, when prayers brought blessed respite. The day then passed with drills and skills. Climbing the masthead, furling and unfurling the sails, practising with swords. Dinner at noon. At 1 p.m., the boys divided into working parties—one for gun drill, one for seamanship, and one for school—until supper at 5.00. Half an hour later, they were hard at it again until 7.30, when the order came to 'stand by your hammocks' for inspection. Edward and his new friends could rest their tired muscles until lights out at 8.30.

Edward was a survivor. He learned the shipboard routines promptly and was nippy about the deck to avoid the cane that cut the backs of the sluggish. The day was broken up into long sessions: physical exercises and training drills; cleaning and inspections; lessons in reading and writing, spelling and dictation, arithmetic, history, geography, and religion; and finally, prayers. On Sundays, God provided relief. Edward could sleep in until 5.30. Then there were only light work duties before Divine Service at 10.00 a.m. and Sunday School at 1.00 p.m. From 2.30, he was at liberty to read or write letters or play quiet board games—but no cards, dice, or gambling of any sort. In winter, the pace slackened—the day's work started late at 6.30 a.m. and ended early at 8 p.m.

The commander applied strict rules in training the boys to 'diligence, assiduity and good conduct'. If Edward was insolent he was put on a diet of bread and water. If negligent with his clothes, hammock, or bag he was ordered to carry those items on his shoulders for an hour at a time. Punishments for minor offences were not to exceed three days. More serious offences like disobeying an order led to solitary confinement—not to exceed seven days. In cases of 'very daring disobedience' caning would not exceed six strokes and was done in front of all the boys as a warning to them all. Whipping for theft and 'highly immoral' behaviour was not to exceed 24 lashes. On the other hand, the commander granted privileges such as extra leave to boys who earned good conduct badges (*Victoria Government Gazette* No. 150 24/10/1865: 2467–74).

Edward found the training increasingly arduous because the never-ending inflow of new inmates left no room to swing a ship's cat. On St Valentine's Day 1868, to ease the congestion, Edward and some other boys were moved to the *Nelson*, a newly acquired hulk moored off Williamstown.

When launched by royalty on the Thames in 1814, *The Nelson* was a smart new battleship of 126 guns and served at Waterloo. The boys were told it was a matter of great pride, that this man-o'-war was their new home. They should feel privileged, but Edward was not seduced by that speechifying. In the dead of night on 7 May 1868, he slid silently overboard. Could it be mere coincidence that at the same time Isaac Brailsford, Edward's fellow escapee from Sunbury three years earlier, made his escape from the *Sir Harry Smith* (*Argus* 8/1/1869: 7)?

Under the headline, 'Deserters from H.M. Service', the *VPG* (14/5/1868: 190) described Edward as '…age 14, 4 feet 10 inches high, light hair, blue eyes; wore serge frock & trousers over suit of duck, all numbered 7, & cap with ribbon marked 'Naval Training Ship'. A month later, the *VPG* carried a second notice of Edward's escape, and in the process, raised his age by a year and his height by two inches. The notice alerted police that Edward was likely to head for Ballarat, where he'd first been sentenced in February 1865. The tip-off proved accurate. He was captured in Ballarat East in January 1869 (*VPG* 28/1/1869: 21) living off his wits again among the street urchins of Ballarat and Geelong. He had been at large for nine months. Before this second escape, Edward had been due for release in February 1869; but as a repeat absconder, he was awarded an extra year in this juvenile gaol (*Argus* 26/1/1869: 16). The system that was designed to rescue and reform children served to criminalise many of them.

Who knows why Edward absconded? We know that the conditions at Sunbury were disgusting, but ship life took brutality to another level. A Royal Commission reported that the system 'is hurtful to the health, the morals, and the intellectual and industrial training of the children, and tends to sink them in after-life into permanent pauperism and crime' (Victoria 1870: vii). Another Royal Commission into Penal and Prison Discipline a few years later confirmed the situation:

> *Experience too clearly proves that immoral practices of the worst kind spring up amongst them which can never be effectually suppressed…The associations with ship life, also induce…an unsettled and roving disposition… (Argus* 19/8/1872: 6).

In that all-male environment was Edward ever subjected to 'immoral practices of the worst kind'? In later life, Edward's friend, Isaac Brailsford, fulfilled the expectation of sinking into 'after-life into permanent pauperism and crime'. Using official sources, I tracked him through the prison system at Ballarat, Geelong, Pentridge, the Battery, and another rotten prison hulk, the *Sacramento*, lying in Hobson's Bay near the *Deborah* where he had spent some of his institutional life seven years earlier (Brogden 2000: 63). After almost 20 years of multiple incarcerations, Isaac was finally released from Pentridge Gaol in 1883—the best years of his life stolen from him for the sake of six ducks. Edward had taken a different path.

6

A wedding despite the shotgun

In February 1870, after five lost years, Edward Sinnett was discharged from the *Nelson*. He was placed in an apprenticeship with his violent stepfather, the butcher Richard Stokes. Neither master nor apprentice was happy with this arrangement. Edward couldn't forget that it was this bully who had battered him and his mother without mercy, had humiliated him by advertising an insulting reward for his capture when he ran away, and had finally 'given him in to custody' (*Star* 7/2/1865: 4). On the other hand, Stokes was in no position to argue. During Edward's incarceration, he had fallen well in arrears in payments the court had ordered to be paid to the Welfare, and feared the penalty that so far had not been applied. Stokes was not keen to have his wife's black sheep back in his home. He had his own children now. Previously, Edward had been named as the oldest sibling on the birth certificates of each of the new Stokes children, but after his return to the family, he was now omitted from the birth certificates of all later siblings.

Readers can be confident that Edward saw to it that his mother wasn't abused again. He was now a strapping 16 and Stokes was approaching 60. In deference to his mother, Edward did what he could to be civil to Stokes, even tolerating being named Edward Stokes in and around his stepfather's butchering business. But it was an uneasy truce, and Edward found every pretext to get away from his company. As soon as he could claim his freedom from his indenture, he found work on Mr Kemp's farm at Soldier's Hill in Ballarat. What's more, he had found a young woman who had taken a shine to him—Alice Watson of Buninyong—and they planned to marry.

Three months before the wedding, set for 31 March 1879, Edward and some friends arranged to go on a hunting expedition, shooting opossums. They rode a spring cart for two days to Kinypanial, a tiny settlement in wild scrub country near the old gold-mining town of Inglewood in central Victoria. They pitched a tent, and yarned around the campfire well into the night. On New Year's Day, perhaps a little the worse for wear after the revelry, Edward loaded his double-barrelled fowling piece, incorrectly. When he fired it, one barrel burst. It shattered his left hand and severely lacerated his face. His friends rushed him to Rickards' Hotel (a Cobb & Co coach stop). Seeing the urgency, Mr Rickards at once drove him by horse and cart to the Inglewood Hospital. Dr. Snowball, the acting hospital surgeon, amputated Edward's hand above the wrist. The Bendigo *Advertiser*, the newspaper closest to the accident, reported that young man (naming him Sinnett) was 'progressing favorably' (3/1/1879: 3). By contrast, the Geelong *Advertiser* had 'the poor fellow… in such a critical condition that it is impossible to move him at present' (Geelong *Advertiser* 7/1/1879: 3).

The Ballarat *Courier* had picked up the story, and gave it a new take. It interviewed Edward's family and, contrary to the Bendigo and Geelong papers, reported the victim's name as Edward Stokes, 'twenty-three years of age, whose parents reside on the Main road, Ballarat.' The Ballarat paper had more to report than the accident with the gun. It was scathing about the reaction of a 'near relative'.

> *We cannot but condemn the heartless conduct of a near relative of the injured man, who, when informed of the accident on Satur-*

> *day, exclaimed "It served him right," at the same time using more emphatic language, in gloating over the unfortunate occurrence. The only regret is that the bystanders did not dip the unfeeling fellow in a horse-trough (Courier* 6/1/1879: 2; reproduced in Bendigo *Advertiser* 9/1/1879: 3).

It's not hard to guess to the identity of the 'near relative'—this 'unfeeling fellow'. Edward would be soon rid of him—and shed the name Stokes for all time. He was soon well enough to proceed with the marriage to Alice at the end of March as planned. Alice wouldn't hear of postponing the wedding and certainly not its cancellation. She'd already made her gown. The community rallied to his support. Friends were still chipping in after the wedding at fundraising concerts in May and June (Bacchus Marsh *Express* 31/5/1879: 3; 14/6/1879: 3). At the first concert, Edward was persuaded to sing in front of an audience of more than 300 people, and they asked for an encore. The second event raised a handsome sum and 'the room having been cleared, dancing was begun and kept up till morning'. Edward was no longer 'the lad who lost his arm through the bursting of a gun', and no longer the stepson of the bullying Stokes. He was a married man who was expected now to be a breadwinner and provider. With one arm, he was not confident he could make ends meet.

With her dressmaking skills, they wouldn't starve, although when eight babies arrived in quick succession between 1883 and 1894 (three of the babies died), there wasn't much time for Alice's dressmaking. Edward was grateful when the Chennery family gave him some occasional work in their corner store in Clayton Street in Ballarat East. He and Alice and his children were able to live in the tiny cottage attached to the store. Unlike the perpetual pauper Isaac Beresford, his runaway friend, Edward was never incarcerated again, nor was he ever totally destitute, although from time to time he faced the courts for unpaid debts.

Permella Sinnett first met her father-in-law ten years after the second accident that blew three fingers off his 'good' hand. She could sense the depth of the scars of his childhood even when he joked about his stupidity in the Guy Fawkes fireworks mishap (Index to Goldfields Hospital Admissions: 17/7/1905, 6/11/1905). The loss of his arm was a constant reminder of his stepfather, the long departed but never lamented Richard Stokes who mocked his misfortune at the time of his accident. Stokes had died in 1884, but Edward could never forgive the man who beat him and his mother and caused him to squander his youth in the emotional wasteland of the juvenile penal system. Such was Edward's esteem around town that he received funds from a benefit event held at the close of the Ballarat Exhibition in 1906 (Geelong *Advertiser* 10/4/1906: 4).

Like many an institutionalised child, Edward had never known the love of a nurturing family. He had never seen any man showing affection to a child. In turn, he found it hard to show love to his children. That's not to say he didn't love them, but as the years went by and his children grew older and more self-reliant, Edward seemed to find it ever more difficult to speak to them. He rarely spoke to them of his cruel incarceration as a child. He was ashamed of the part he played in his own loss of childhood. He may not have known about the way his father had died, but he never told his family. The emotional baggage of being the unwanted outsider in the Stokes household stayed with him. He volunteered very little even to Alice.

Edward respected Alice for being competent in everything she did. Over time, the energy and capability of his wife became sufficient for the household, and his own role shrank even further. He sat for days at a time without feeling the necessity to speak to anyone. To the casual observer, Edward seemed past caring about life, but there was plenty to occupy his mind with his offspring setting tongues wagging in the town.

PART 3
THE GREAT WAR

The instructors' faces were set in a permanent ghastly grin. 'Hurt him, now! In at the belly! Tear his guts out!' they would scream, as the men charged the dummies. 'Now the upper swing at his privates with the butt. Ruin his chances for life! No more little Fritzes!...Naaoh! Anyone would think that you loved the bloody swine, patting and stroking 'em like that! BITE HIM, I SAY! STICK YOUR TEETH IN HIM AND WORRY HIM! EAT HIS HEART OUT!'

— Robert Graves, 1929

7

Joining up

I like to think my mother's mother Permella Adams and her father Billy Sinnett was classic love-at-first-sight. I picture a Saturday night dance at Ballarat Town Hall in 1915. Billy is 20 and Permella 18. He dresses to impress, immaculate in a dark navy-blue three-piece suit with a winged collar and red silk tie. I can see him taking off his slick brown hat in the cloakroom. Flicking back his brilliantined hair. Looking about him to see who's watching. Permella Adams wouldn't have lowered her eyes.

When I was young, I met Permella more times than I can count. Now, decades after her death, I find it hard to conjure up an image of her face. I've never seen a photograph of her but I have seen photos of my mother and her sister Minnie as young women, and if Permella looked like her daughters, I imagine she could readily turn a young man's head. In soldier lingo, a bit of 'eyes right.' As a teenager, she was a domestic servant six days a week, and would have known her place in polite society. But it's easy to imagine her breaking free on a Saturday night. The second-last in her large family, she would have been assertive among her own crowd. She would make the Saturday night dance floor at the Town Hall her domain. Bright-eyed, animated, confident and outgoing. No mistress here to tell her to pull up her stockings. No master to leer at her as she poured the tea. No spoilt brat to tug the bell to summon her from the kitchen just to show he could. The gossips might have said she knew far more than her prayers. She could cope with this cocky young Sinnett.

Within months, on 30 June 1915, they were married at the Sinnetts' customary place of union, the Ballarat Town and City Mission. The Mission was accustomed to spur-of-the-moment weddings with expectant brides. The Sinnetts were regular patrons. As a youngster, Billy had a front-row seat at his siblings' courtships, couplings, and abundance of babies. This was an age when adults minded their tongues because, to use one of my mother's favourite expressions, 'Little pitchers have big ears'. Billy's worldly knowledge came not from what he heard, but what he saw. He was just twelve when his oldest sister, Lilly (then 21), married Stephen Coombes (22) in 1906 and began to produce nine children. Billy's second sister, Minnie (20), already had a child (in January 1910) before she married Herbert Allen (19) in 1911. Minnie and Herbert then had twin girls, followed by four more children in quick succession. Hilda Constance (18) was Billy's third, and favourite, sister. Connie was, as they used to say, 'with child' in 1912 when she married Harry Matheson. Harry was not yet 16 and you can imagine the whispers about the father of Connie's child.

Billy learned about death, too, at close hand. Three of his brothers died in infancy, and his sister Lilly buried her twin sons and a daughter all before their second birthday. His oldest brother Sam buried his third child at just seven months in 1913—just before my mother was born. Billy knew the couplings of pleasure and pain, and life and death.

Billy and Permella were born for each other if the family symmetry meant anything. Each was the eighth child out of nine in their families. Both sets of parents—Edward and Alice Sinnett and David and Catherine Adams—had their first child in 1883 and their last child in 1898. Both fathers had been miners in Ballarat. The divine power of numbers.

Despite their ages, he 20 and she 18, their parents' consent would not have been hard to win. My mother was already, by then, more than a glint in her parent's eyes. Alice Sinnett was not warm towards her new daughter-in-law. To be 'in the family way' after so brief a courtship told her all she needed to know. Edward Sinnett, by contrast, was happy to have another son reach manhood and be 'off his hands.' With one arm amputated and only the pointer and thumb on his 'good' hand, Edward liked to get in first with that joke. At their wedding he was barely able to make his mark of consent. Disqualified from mining, Edward now granted himself the title farmer, although it is hard to imagine how a man with one arm and only two remnant digits on the other could make a living on the land.

Wednesday weddings at the Mission went unreported. David Adams, Permella's father, had no money for a showy wedding. The gold mining boom was over in Ballarat, and he earned an irregular income as a carter. Billy's father couldn't contribute either. He'd already been before the courts twice for defaulting on debts (VPRS 290/PO). The couple started married life with nothing more than tenderness.

As she lay in Billy's arms by candlelight, Permella's fingers traced the tattooed dragon down his left forearm to the back of his hand. She discovered Billy's fascination with men of action and all things military. As a child, Billy looked not to his father as hero, but to his oldest brother, Samuel, eleven years his senior. Sam took him to shooting competitions on a Saturday. From the station at Ballarat East, Billy leaned his head out from the train as it steamed through the viaduct under busy Victoria Street and zipped past the Eureka Siding to York Street and Levy (called Spencer Street Station until city folk said it was confusing to have two stations of the same name). From the Butts Station at Clayton, it was a hop and a skip to the rifle range.

Billy carried Sam's old rifle. Once, when the captain turned a blind eye, Billy shot three rounds from 100 yards and managed two outers and an inner. No bull, Sam said, but not bad for a little tacker. In competitions, Sam shot as tenth and last man. The best rifleman shot last, Billy told Permella. Permella noticed that Billy's dragon tattoo was identical to the one that ran down Sam's arm.

Billy loved to re-tell Sam's tales of audacity, death, and glory in the Boer War in South Africa. Permella listened attentively enough, but she thought it far-fetched. When he was aged 24, Sam shifted to Tasmania, and Billy had been distraught. There, for reasons he did not disclose to Billy, Sam changed his name to Henry Marshall Sinnett and married Annie May Ryan in March 1908, just in time for a son, George Henry, to be born in June. They had another boy, Leslie Raymond, a few years later (in 1910), and then moved to Bacchus Marsh. Sam kept in touch with the Sinnetts of Ballarat—but at a distance.

Billy couldn't match Sam's Boer War stories, and nor did Permella have many stories to share. Girls were not meant to have adventures. Her brothers allowed her to play with them on condition she chased after the balls they hit to test the long grass for snakes. Girls like her grew up indoors, found jobs as maids or serving girls until they got married and had children—not always in that order. When she was 14, a young man at Haddon fell off his horse and appeared hurt. Permella, walking nearby, grabbed the reins and tied the mare to a tree. She made the man as comfortable as she could and, although she'd never ridden a horse before, somehow reached his parents' house to raise the alarm. The hospital said his skull was fractured and, but for her prompt action, he would have died. The young man's father gave her a guinea and wrote her a letter of recommendation, which gained her a job with a well-to-do family in Ballarat. However, it had not been easy working for rude people, she said. She was on her third job already when she met Billy.

Permella should have known that Billy was destined to leave her for the war. In his spare time, he was already wearing the uniform of the Ballarat-based 70th Australian Infantry Regiment—the 'Saturday afternoon soldiers', some called them. He'd joined as soon as he was old enough. Compulsory military training started in 1911, but Billy hadn't needed to be conscripted. He was a true believer, schooled on the newspaper articles that became the best-selling *Deeds that Won the Empire,* by Ballarat's own Dr Fitchett. Britain was our mother and our protector. If the Japanese, the Germans, or the Russians poked their noses into our region, the best navy in the world from the very best country in the world would come to the rescue. The call to action had come in the middle of the election of 1914—no better time to beat the patriotic drums with talk of defending the Empire 'to our last man and our last shilling' (Warhaft 2004: 74).

When the mother country declared war on Germany on 4 August 1914, Billy was proud to be with the Militia Regiment garrisoned at Queenscliff at the entrance to Port Phillip Bay. The men cheered the news that Australia had offered an infantry division of 20 000 men. It would never have entered Billy's head to shirk his duty, but he had seen boys and young men, even some of his acquaintances, using dirty tricks to dodge their compulsory training. That was not his way, he assured Permella. A great war would be fought in Europe, and Australia would be there. He would be there. He must be, just as Sam had been in South Africa.

Billy had seen scores of men queuing up at the recruiting centre in Ballarat. All around him, his pals in Ballarat were enlisting: Jimmy Morton and Reggie Clark from Sebastopol, Charlie Davis from Main Road, Percy Cooper from Humffray Street, John Nelson from Victoria Street, and Bertie Brudenell, a boy from the Orphanage. Billy knew them all. They had signed up for the 'great adventure', so why not him?

Billy would have heard the whispers of cowardice—perhaps even felt the cold shoulder from a girl who had once been his friend. Men formed an association in Melbourne and wore a badge on their coat lapels to show that they had volunteered but had been rejected (Scott 1936: 209n). Billy could not bear the prospect of being insulted by a white feather in the post. It was not his fault that he had not sailed for the battlefield long before this. His fists tightened whenever he had to explain. He was five feet four inches, but the Army insisted that a soldier must be five feet six. Two inches, for goodness' sake! He read that the British cut their height requirements in February 1915, from five feet eight inches to just five feet, and an extra 50 000 men joined up straight away—the 'Bantam Battalions' they were called. Billy could hold a rifle better than any six-footer. His two and a half years in the 70th Infantry in Ballarat and tuition from big brother Sam had made him a crack shot. The AIF must come to their senses, he said.

Billy had been furious when Harry Matheson, the husband of his sister Connie, joined up in September 1914. Harry was the first of the family to enlist. He was a naïve boy among real men, but he was tall enough to fight for God and Empire whereas Billy, with all his fervour, could not. Height was one thing, intelligence another. Harry thought you needed your parents' approval if you were under 20 (it was 21) so he put his age up to 20. Not only was he wrong about that, but he didn't know that married men didn't need parental consent—or the consent of wives, for that matter. Australian wives didn't share Canadian wives' right to veto their husbands' enlistment.

Just a few weeks before Permella and Billy married, the AIF declared that they would lower the height prerequisite to five feet two inches. Billy now was in—with two inches to spare. As a married man, like Harry, he no longer needed his father's approval to enlist. Did an uneasy thought lodge in Permella's brain? Did Billy know all along what he was doing when he asked her to marry him? Surely, he wouldn't have been so manipulative.

Was it too late to dissuade him? Permella would have put her position with passion. Sneerers targeted single men, but people understood a married man hesitating, especially with a baby on the way. They needed to get to know each other better as man and wife and soon to be mother and father. This was a faraway war, not our battle. Those who started the stoush should sort out their squabbles for themselves. It was barefaced hypocrisy for a Christian nation to wage war on a nation thousands of miles over the other side of the world. Billy rejected all her fancy talk.

Permella showed him the newspaper stories that said the initial enthusiasm for the war was waning. More than 10 000 volunteers had come forward in January 1915, but by April, the monthly recruitment figure had dropped to just over 6 000. Early in May, the newspaper reports of appalling numbers killed and maimed at Gallipoli renewed her hope that her man would see the light.

The tales of tragedy may have deterred some from

enlisting, but the tales of heroism inspired Billy all the more. Turning the argument about heavy casualties on its head, he reckoned it showed how much more he and thousands of extra volunteers were now needed. His case was proved, he said, when the volunteer numbers began to rise again—over 10 000 volunteers in May, more than 12 500 in June, and in July, numbers trebled to 36 575—more than half of them from Victoria. This was the greatest number for any month of the whole war (Robson 1970: 54). Ballarat employers added their names to the published lists of companies willing to 'liberate' their employees who wanted to volunteer and, 'on their return, to reinstate them in the positions they occupied prior to enlisting' (Ballarat *Courier* 14/7/1915).

Permella's determination to keep her man home was under fire on all fronts. After their wedding, they moved in with Billy's parents at Chennery's Store in Clayton Street, close to the rifle butts at Levy. The racket of rifle fire was an everyday reminder that pals of Billy were training within earshot. To make matters worse, just two days after Billy and Permella were married, Sam Sinnett announced that he had joined up (under his new name, Henry) and, on the basis of being a Boer war veteran and a nurse in a mental asylum, he was immediately given the rank of corporal. He was keen to lead the way, he said.

Permella fought not just against Billy and his family and friends, but the entire machine of national sentiment. Pro-war emotion was broadcast everywhere—in churches, offices, and factories, and in schools, shops, and pubs. Men surged to the enlistment centres; families named their newborn babies 'Anzac' (Reid 2002: 138). Almost all newspaper editors ran with the government-inspired propaganda. The local paper ran a story called the 'Sermonette' and invoked

Numbers xxxii: 23: 'Be sure your sins will find you out.'

> *The sin of our text is the sin of shirking one's duty in a time of war...The Almighty continually resorts to physical means to achieve moral ends. One of these physical means is war, and man is the medium of its administration (Courier:* 27/2/1915: 7).

Billy's mother had no need to invoke God. Six bob a day and all found, she argued, where can you get good money like that in Ballarat these days? Yes, they could do with the money, Permella conceded, but Billy wouldn't be just some tourist. He'd be no good to anyone if he went to an early grave. Their child would be born an orphan.

When Billy walked in the door and announced that he had just been accepted, just three weeks after their wedding, his mother hugged him close, but Permella turned her back to slice the bread, and set the table in icy silence. After tea, she told the family her pregnancy was making her tired and went to bed early. Billy hardly noticed. He had to tell his father and young Syd about his new Lee Enfield rifle. You could load a five-round clip of 303-inch calibre ammunition into the magazine and kill a man more than two miles away.

Billy's enlistment was completed on 26 July 1915, and he was assigned to the 22nd Battalion, with the regimental number 2047. He'd signed up as William Frank Sinnett, discarding his third name 'Salvador.' He knew that aliens were treated with suspicion as the enemy within, and many were interned. He felt sorry for Fritz Grigoliet, a former inmate of the Ballarat Orphanage, and a decent man. Fritz had been given such a hard time in training camp that he deserted. He later re-enlisted using the alias Frederick Bone, while his brother, Hendrick, enlisted as Henry Woods.

Private Sinnett was now impatient. He'd learned enough

with the militia. All any Australian soldier needs is to see a Hun, squeeze the trigger and shoot the bastard. When you've shot enough bastards, the war's over and we come home quick smart. Sam had seen the Boers in South Africa. Bushmen with a keen eye. Crack shots, all of them. Used rifles in everyday life before the war. Australians could be even better. They could take their place in the battle line a week or two after getting their rifles.

High command wasted no time getting reinforcements to the front. A month after Private Billy Sinnett enlisted—and just 56 days after his wedding—he embarked at Melbourne on the troop transport *Anchises*, bound for his great adventure. Three days out to sea he turned 21.

Permella did her best to hide her feelings as he set off to the station with the rest of the family. She pleaded morning sickness, but like her pregnancy—now four months along—some things were obvious. Billy felt the cool sarcasm in her promise to put away his wedding suit until he got home. He told her he would be home for Christmas. It would be all over in a wink. Billy thought it churlish that she hadn't made the trip to Port Melbourne, but on board the *Anchises*, he was pleased to find a sprig of rosemary in his kit with a note about ancient Greeks wearing rosemary in their hair to strengthen their memory. Billy would find rosemary aplenty on the bloody hills of Gallipoli.

8

Connie and Harry

Permella Sinnett was free of Alice Sinnett when Billy's sister, Hilda Constance Sinnett, now Connie Matheson asked her to move in to her house in York Street. Permella helped with Connie's children—Thomas, nearly three, and Mavis, just a few months old. Connie was fun. She had a repertoire of intimate stories about her life with her boy husband Harry before he left for the War. They would be two single women with plenty of diversions. Permella could laugh again.

In 1912, Hilda Constance Sinnett had married Harry Matheson at the Ballarat Registry. In view of her condition, their parents had readily consented though she was just 18, and he was barely 15 (but claimed to be 16). Many who knew Connie doubted Harry was the father of her child.

Once married, Connie was blunt. Harry had served his purpose. She now urged him to serve the higher purpose of God, King and Empire. He was among the first in Ballarat to enlist—in September 1914, claiming to be nearly 19 when in fact he was just 17. However, he seemed incapable of getting on a troopship to go to the war. It's quite a story—or rather, two stories. His long letter to the AIF dated 21/7/1920 tells one version; a detailed report of his evidence in his divorce proceedings tells a different one (*Courier* 6/6/1920). From his AIF dossier it's possible to construct a truthful—if complicated—narrative.

Harry had been sent to training camp at Broadmeadows with the 8th Battalion, Ballarat's own and the AIF deemed him ready for battle in October 1914. Had he embarked, as ordered, on HMAT *Benalla* on the 19th of that month, he would have been among the first Anzacs at what became the historic landing at Gallipoli the following April. But Harry had other things on his mind.

On the Saturday before sailing, Harry said he heard a rumour about Connie. He dashed back to Ballarat, ready for battle. Hardly in the door, he shot off a rhetorical question: 'Have you been carrying on with another man?' Taking silence as a yes, Harry fired off a second shot: 'Were you drunk in the presence of this man?' Gaining no response, he shot off a third and final round: 'What's the bastard's name, then?' Constance was in no mood to be challenged by this adolescent. Provoked by his aggression, she let fly some invective of her own, accompanied by her wedding ring, which struck him flush on the temple. 'I'll get the father of the child to keep him. If you don't like it, you can lump it.'

Harry missed the last train back to Melbourne on the Sunday and had to wait for the first train on Monday morning. By then, the 8th Battalion had already embarked. He'd missed the boat, and with it death or glory at Gallipoli. The 8th Battalion would land at a small cove (named Anzac Cove after the war) on 25 April 1915 (now Anzac Day). Within ten days, almost a third of the unit's men were killed or wounded. Many of the survivors were later killed at Lone Pine.

Back in Australia, Harry had vanished—for four months if you believe the explanation he gave to the AIF at the end of the War; or for 20 months if you believe his evidence at his divorce hearing shortly thereafter. Understanding his documented military career requires concentration. After missing the boat in 1914, Harry faced a dilemma. He was a deserter in effect, and feared being arrested. On the other hand, if he returned to the AIF, the disgraceful Connie would get his military allotment. His solution was to re-enlist, but present himself as a new recruit. When 'James Allen' joined up on 19 February 1915, he said he was a single man nearly 21 years of age. (Harry was, in fact, 17 years and eight months.) 'James Allen' produced a letter purporting to be from Mrs Charlotte Allen of Lydiard Street, Ballarat, his mother and next-of-kin. He had been inspired by his mother's listed as Charlotte Smith on his marriage certificate in 1912. As a new recruit allocated to the 23rd Battalion, Private Allen was sent to the training camp at Broadmeadows. His battalion was due to sail out in March 1915. He was still not too late to fight at Gallipoli—had he made it. However, he was taken ill with measles and confined to the military hospital. While he was in the sick bay, his unit sailed without him, again, leaving Harry Matheson stranded in Australia for the second time. Later, he claimed falsely that after recovering from measles, he had been given a week's leave. The AIF never saw 'James Allen' again.

In July 1915, feeling the pressure from those who saw him skulking around Ballarat, Harry Matheson volunteered for a third time. This time he called himself 'Andrew Leslie Matheson'. He described himself as a single man, and nominated his mother as next-of-kin. This time his mother was not Charlotte Smith but Mrs J Matheson of 53 Victoria Street. The month before, his older brother, John Rodney Matheson, had enlisted saying his mother was Mrs G Canty of 53 Victoria Street. I'm not sure if the boys' mother knew what they were doing in her name(s).

By now, the real Harry Matheson had just celebrated his 18th birthday, but his new persona, Andrew Matheson, claimed to be 21 and 4 months, so he did not need a real or fictional mother to consent to his enlistment. Andrew Matheson didn't have a long military career. He was discharged in September 1915 after just two months as unfit for service because he dislocated his knee in training. That much, at least, is probably a fact. But years later, Harry Matheson was still lying. He told the AIF that as Andrew Matheson, he had been arrested and court-martialled for desertion. There was no such court-martial in the military records.

Meanwhile in the midst of this turmoil, on 21 December 1915, Permella gave birth to Hilda Frances Sinnett, my mother, named in honour of Hilda Constance Matheson (but in later life, my mother was always called Frances or Fran). Permella found life with the new baby and with Connie was not always exciting and amusing. She had to put up with Harry Matheson's erratic appearances. He sometimes came in uniform and sometimes not, but he was always quarrelsome and aggressive. He often upset Permella's baby and Connie's small children.

If it wasn't Harry keeping the house awake, it was Connie's baby, Mavis, crying day and night with stomach cramps. Permella, a first-time single mother, had expected to rely on Connie's experience to help her learn how to cope with a new-born child, but Connie was in no fit state to extend a helping hand when her own child was so troubled. In February 1916, with some misgivings, Permella decided she should retreat to her parents' house in Ripon Street. Her baby was just two months old.

A few weeks later, a message arrived from Connie asking Permella to come quickly. By the time she arrived, baby Mavis had died of gastroenteritis. Permella felt ashamed that she had left Connie at the time of her greatest need.

The death of baby Mavis, who may (or may not) have been his daughter, might have brought Harry Matheson to his senses—for a time at least. Or maybe it was all too much for him. In April 1916, he went back to the recruitment office—the same place where he had already signed up as Harry Matheson, James Allen, and Andrew Matheson. This time, he didn't bother with an alias. He assumed, correctly, that the AIF would be too concerned with getting able-bodied men to the front to recognise that they were getting just one soldier for the price of four. In this, his quadruplicate enlistment, he named Connie as his next-of-kin and gallantly arranged for an allotment from his pay.

However, it was a brief ceasefire: by the time he finally embarked in July 1916, he had nominated a new next-of-kin, a Mr Bond, a friend with whom he had been living when Connie kicked him out. Mr Bond's daughter, Ethel, was much more his kind of girl—as would be revealed later. Whether using his real name or James Allen or Andrew Leslie Matheson, Harry had obviously taken some pleasures at home before he sailed. His 40 days at sea were spent in the troopship's hospital with the euphemistic 'social disease'. Despite enlisting a year earlier than Billy Sinnett, Harry didn't finally disembark in England until September 1916, by which time Billy had already fought at Gallipoli and the Somme, and was lucky to be still alive.

9

The great adventure

Billy Sinnett had been three days out to sea in August 1915 when he turned 21. On board the *Anchises* he had more to think about than his birthday. It was his first time at sea and he was captivated by the grand excursion.

Permella kept Billy's well-thumbed letter in her apron pocket. 'Take care what you write in your letters home,' the officers warned the men; 'we will read everything.' There were things Billy preferred not to tell Permella, anyway. He wouldn't mention the lecture warning them against the excesses of the flesh and how to avoid venereal disease. Nor would he mention that the advice was already too late for a few men: some spent most of the journey in the ship's hospital, laid up by syphilis caught long before they set foot on foreign soil.

Permella knew many of the men on board. Several were from Ballarat and Billy had knocked around with them or knew their faces on the streets: Peter Davis, Claude Schaefer, Gus Stelling, John Redfern, and Dave Tait. John Matheson was there too, the older brother of Harry, Connie's husband. John Matheson was with the 21st Battalion, separated from the 22nd, which suited Billy.

Billy was thrown together with others he didn't know, too, but they would be friends in no time. They all kipped in hammocks on the open decks. On one side of him were the Smith brothers, George and Percy, from Wartook. On his other side were Hughie Kelly from Fitzroy and Jimmy Morton from Skipton Street. He envied Jimmy's regimental number 2000, so easy to remember. Living in the excitement of the moment, Billy could never imagine that some of these men would never see Australia again.

Billy told Permella they were woken every morning at seagull fart and were soon dripping with sweat. Fitness drills every morning. Running on the spot, push-ups, scaling rope ladders, boxing, obstacle races made even more challenging as the ship pitched and rolled. In the afternoons, they sat in the sun half-listening to lectures about infantry tactics and how they should behave in Egypt.

When the *Anchises* reached the mouth of the Canal, Billy was exhilarated by the sight of the many vessels lined up waiting to go through in convoy. When the big lighthouse showing a red and a white light at the entrance to the Gulf of Suez came into view, the cheers were deafening. The officers turned a blind eye to the revelry that night. Next morning, there were a few grumpy heads, but they packed themselves into the train to Zeitoun. From there, they marched all the way to Heliopolis with full kit and heavy packs. Passing camp after camp, Billy saw Australian troops down to singlets and shorts basking in the hot sun. He slept well that night.

His next letter to Permella described the camp in the desert near Cairo and Heliopolis. A man could want for nothing—billiard saloons, wet and dry canteens, ice cream stalls; but he could do without the flies and sand in his mouth, unbearable heat, and surly officers. They could get into Cairo occasionally, he added. Dirty, dark alleyways, native stalls, cripples and beggars—letter writers were less politically correct than we are today. There were topics that could've made your mother blush. Women sat in doorways lifting up their clothes to show themselves and called out, 'Very clean, very nice.' The upper-class brothels were in a place called the Yser—if a bloke was looking. Permella must have wondered if her bloke was looking when gossip started to come through. Free from the constraints of family responsibilities, away from wives and girlfriends, thousands of AIF men did more than take a look. More than 3 400 Australian soldiers contracted VD in Egypt in 1915 (Stanley 2011: 30.)

Billy had not expected still more training. He thought he was ripe for a crack at the Turks after all the training in Ballarat and Broadmeadows and then on board ship. However, here in the face of mounting casualties shipped in from Gallipoli, the message was becoming clear. It's not a simple matter of pointing your rifle at the Turks quicker than they point theirs at you. Only disciplined soldiers stay alive. So reveille was at 0430 ('That's 4.30 in the morning,' he explained). Mug of tea at 0515. Parade at 0600. Physical jerks, then breakfast and a spell. Indoor instruction in the huts. Musketry. Tucker at 1230. Bayonet practice. Dig a trench in the soft sand. Fill it in. Dig again. The uniform was too heavy—the temperature was always above 90ºF. A break from the sapping heat: cards or two-up, or a catnap. Parade again from 1630–1730. Night marches. Lectures: how to occupy and hold an entrenched position. All Billy wanted was to be let loose on Johnny Turk.

During that first week, he would have been surprised to see so many men sick—diarrhoea, heatstroke, septic hands, knees, and feet. And ophthalmia, of all things. His father had seen boys die of it in the industrial schools in Melbourne and Sunbury. Now, close to the scene, the thought occurred: there was some prospect that he would never see Permella again, or his brothers and sisters.

Like many others, he made the most of the opportunities to go over the top in Egypt. He poked around Cairo with pals from the *Anchises*. He was as rigorous as any military censor in editing letters to Permella. He did not tell her that he had sold his camera to cover his two-up losses. It was simpler to say—with a faint ring of truth—that it went missing in action.

At times, Billy moped about why Permella hadn't made a bigger effort to see him off at the pier. He regretted the suddenness of their separation. Their short time together had been so happy, and he missed her more than he thought he would. He was pleased when his paybook was brought up-to-date and he saw that she was being looked after. He would be paid the princely sum of six bob a day (about $27)—more money than he got at home if he counted the days lost to rain. He was allowed to draw a bob a week, and another bob was put aside as savings. Permella was allotted the rest. That was a load off his mind at least. With a baby on the way, Permella wouldn't be able to work, even if she could find a job. When the baby arrived, she was entitled to another 1/9½d a week. Every little bit would help, he thought, but who would have imagined that the cost of food in Australia would increase by nearly 45 per cent during the War (*Argus* 22/5/1919: 6)?

Permella would have read his letters again, looking for some sign that Billy was missing her or that he appreciated how lonely she was. So much for rosemary in his kit. It was all very well for him: he had a whole new world to keep him enthralled. But how was she going to survive—a married woman at 18, with a child? How long would it be before she could start living again? Billy would see a bit of the world, a dash of adventure, fight a quick war to pay for all that adventure, then home to Australia to resume normal life—as a married couple, whatever that meant.

On 1st November 1915, Billy sent Permella a hurried postcard from Heliopolis. The battalion was moving out. Couldn't say too much, all hush-hush, lips buttoned. Will be good to get it over and done with. With any luck, he'd be home before the baby arrived.

It was hard for Permella and Billy to keep up to date with the news on either side of the ocean. Letters from home often carried news of events that had long since become out of date. Newspapers published the news from the front well before a letter was delivered at home, although we now know that news cables were not always accurate—sometimes deliberately so. Besides, there was only so much you could say in a letter, not just because of censorship but also also it was impossible to say some things.

Billy had been convinced that Gallipoli would be a walkover, but the closer he came to it, the less sure he became. We know the truth about Gallipoli now, but imagine his excitement and curiosity as his troopship glided into the cove in the strictest silence in the hour between dark and dawn on 26 October 1915. A glimpse of the shore, an occasional light appearing where the beach might be. In the distance, tiny lights twinkled, and an occasional flare glowed orange for a moment in the muddy sky. Excitement gave way to apprehension.

Many soldiers landing as reinforcements have written about making for the beach in lighters and rowing boats at first light. The shock hit when the beach was revealed as a vast rubbish dump: piles of stores and equipment, crates, faded tents, dusty carts, debris from wrecked boats and vehicles, smoke from fires on the beach—dark brown, dull khaki, dreary grey. A dead horse, two hind legs thrust upright, a hole where its front legs should have been. The odour of what could only be rotting flesh mingled with the lingering blue mist of cordite. Men, half-dressed, loaded boxes on to mules. Torn canvas flapped against water flagons.

With the dark sky giving way to dawn, the reinforcements were warned to keep their heads down as they moved forward up a winding path. At a place known as Rest Gully, they organised water and ammunition. The sun was now well up on what seemed a perfect autumn day.

Explosions shattered the calm. Shells burst below on the beach they'd just left. They all ducked for cover, but a sergeant ordered them to move on. Looking ahead, they could see the low spurts of blue and grey smoke from the Turkish lines. Billy had expected the men on the front line to be as excited as he was, but there was no front line, and no enthusiasm. Caked in grime and stale blood, these old hands were dull with fatigue, their clothes grubby, their hair gritty, and their lips tight.

The new men made themselves as comfortable as they could in dugouts on the slopes. Billy would have chosen a possie already scooped out of the side of a small rise, a shallow hole just deep enough to become a grave. He'd been trained for vigorous hand-to-hand skirmishes, and expected to be thrust into gallant bayonet charges, but that kind of fighting was over. Both sides were now deeply entrenched in unsolvable stalemate. The Turks controlled positions overlooking the Australians, who would need to run straight into Turkish machine guns to make any progress. They would have to attack the Turks by digging under them. They could hear the Turks chipping away with their picks, too.

Billy must have expected to see men die at Gallipoli. But it would never have occurred to him that a soldier might die by accident. Mid-afternoon on 29 October, the battalion blew up a mine under the Turkish trenches. An officer climbed down a rope ladder into the tunnel to inspect the effect of the blast. When he failed to return, two men went down with a rope. Only one emerged. Overcome by the carbon dioxide gases lurking in the tunnel, his companion didn't have the strength to climb the ladder. Another engineer went down with two volunteers. All three were asphyxiated. Five men lay dead (Bean 1924 Vol. 2: 201n, 823n).

When the stretcher-bearers passed by with the dead bodies, Billy would have recognised Gus Stelling. They had known each other as boys in Ballarat, had sailed together on the *Anchises*, trained and played together in Egypt, and travelled together to Gallipoli. His parents had given their enthusiastic consent for Gus to go on active service, writing that he would be 'twenty years of age on the 28th of October, 1915'. They couldn't have imagined that their son would be dead the very next day.

The war was not what Billy had imagined. Back home you knew your opponent. You stood up to him fair and square. But here, men hid and waited. Nowhere was safe. As if to prove the point, the Turks bombarded the battalion's position for the next two days and well into the night. Despite the lack of sleep, all men were put on stand-to before dawn. By the time the first dull grey light crept across the battlefield, they were alert and manning their weapons—just in case. Across the line, they could see the Turks putting up barbed wire entanglements even in the face of heavy fire from the Australian guns, including the big guns of the war ships.

The constant barrage from field artillery in both directions created a terrific din.

Billy never really attuned to the war at Gallipoli. The anticipated great adventure had turned into a debacle. Then all the more confusing: the Australians were ordered not to fire unless there was a direct attack against them. A few shells hit the beach, but the Australians made no reply. The next day, the Turks shelled the beach constantly. Again, the Australians made no response. Snow lay on the ground. Men were not allowed to move around. Their fingers and toes went numb.

Historians sometimes write about war as if the killing is all intrepid and heroic. I try to imagine the occasion when Billy Sinnett first killed a man. Did he spot a Turk creeping up close to the trenches? Did he wait until the man was within a few yards? Did he spring forward and thrust his bayonet into his soft guts? Did he see the shock in the man's eyes? Hear the muted gasp as he fell, in slow motion? What do you feel when you've just killed a man? When you've thrust and twisted the blade with all the strength in your wrists? Pulled the blade clear out? Watched the red stain spread across the snow? Heard a man's last gasp? What can you say when you know the man was just a boy like you? Back home, Dr Fitchett's *Deeds that Won the Empire* did not mention that killing a man could traumatise the killer.

Billy wrote nothing of this to Permella. Instead, he told her about the foul weather. Not even the most bitter of Ballarat winter nights matched the Gallipoli storms at the end of November. Sentries clutched their rifles tight, unable to squeeze the trigger if they needed to. One joker said his fingers had mutinied.

On the night of 27 November, the rain came down even

more heavily. The rainwater ran deeper and faster. Little rivulets ran together and swelled to a torrent, pouring into the trenches with increasing speed. Dugouts began to fill. Trench walls broke. Men struggled to get out. Weighed down with heavy gear in the rapidly rising water, some were unable to scale the walls. They drowned like rats. In the cold light of day, the bodies were dragged out of the floodwaters. Many were Turks. Enemy trenches above them had burst under the pressure and the bodies had been flushed down during the black night.

Worse was to come. On the morning of 29 November, the Turks launched the biggest bombardment yet seen on the peninsula. They pummelled for hours, wrecking whole sections of the trenches and supports. Mangled bodies lay everywhere. Men wandered dazed and bewildered, looking for friends, or water. Billy found George Smart, another of the *Anchises* boys, prostrate—his skull fractured. A doctor did what he could, but George died the next morning.

By December, soldiers who reported sick were being evacuated, instead of treated on site. The top brass had decided to end the futility. They were pulling out of Gallipoli. Surely, it was time to go home to Australia? The officers were happy for the men to clean up graves for a couple of hours. It suited their strategy of getting the Turks used to silence without suspecting a retreat. The men would slip away in groups. Billy was among those who would stay till the death.

As darkness fell on 17 December, hundreds of men shuffled off without a sound. Hughie was one of the earliest to leave. He had a raging sore throat and high temperature. Billy's throat had been bad for days, but he hadn't let on how wretched he felt. The queues at the ambulance station were full of men in worse shape than him. How could a man turn up to sick parade with a sore throat?

On the second night, an even larger group moved off down the slopes with strips of torn-up blankets wrapped around their boots to muffle the sound. Nobody spoke. On the night of 19-20 December, the 22nd Battalion evacuated their remaining men in six successive parties. At 2.45 a.m., the last men were ordered off and the evacuation was soon complete, with only a handful of minor casualties—including Billy Sinnett with a wounded ankle. On his way back to Egypt on the hospital ship, *Dunluce Castle,* he knew he was lucky to get out alive. But he grieved over Gus and Percy and Alf. When the reckoning was done, the great adventure had cost the lives of 8 709 Australian men. What could he write to Permella?

At the very time my mother was being born in Ballarat on 21 December 1915, her father was on the hospital ship *Dunluce Castle,* steaming towards Egypt. Permella and Billy would not know their respective news until 1915 had ticked over to 1916. Urgent cables were reserved for more critical matters, and Christmas was a bad time to join the queue if you weren't an officer. At home, women dreaded the approach of a clergyman or a cable. With a baby just three weeks old, Permella feared the worst. Her hands trembled when she opened her cable. She was hysterical, with the laughter that comes with sudden relief, when she read 'sprained ankle'.

Had Permella seen the three reports on Billy's medical condition that I found in his military dossier, she would have been as confused as I was. One report described his injury as 'G.S.W. [gunshot wound] right ankle'. If that was accurate, it meant he was one of the few soldiers wounded during the massive evacuation. A second report said he had both a gunshot wound and a sprained ankle. A third stated that he was admitted with a sprained ankle and bronchitis. Whatever the facts, he was in a bad way. He'd been at Gallipoli for 56 days, but now needed almost as many days again to recover his health. If Permella had been able to see him when he was first admitted to the hospital, she would have been shocked. His clothes were filthy. The nurses had them burned. They had to cut his hair before they could wash off the congealed mud. At Gallipoli, he had washed with half a mug of water and a torn rag. Now, hot water and scented soap were paradise regained. He could shave every day after long sleeps in soft sheets and pyjamas. After ten days of rest, the bronchitis was beginning to clear up. The ankle would take longer. His spirits maybe even longer.

Ships passing in the night carried letters giving the sought-after news. Their daughter had been born at Hilda Constance Matheson's house, hence Hilda. The 'Frances' was no surprise—apparently, they had agreed that had she been a boy she would be Francis. They would have to wait for that.

Gallipoli was done with, and Permella could be forgiven for thinking that her husband would be sent home—and would soon get to see his new daughter. Billy's letter put her right. The retreat from Gallipoli didn't mean the big stoush was over. That's all he knew. Like many letters from the front, his didn't tell her much. He had caught a nasty chest cold, but it was nothing compared with what some of the men had caught—leaving that to her imagination. I imagine that like many soldiers, he had other thoughts too personal to include in a letter that would be read by the censors.

He was hungry for news of his daughter. She was pleased

he asked for another photo of herself if she could manage it. His other one got spoiled in the trenches. Billy thought Permella might have known 'Pompey' Elliott, the colonel who had sailed with him on the hospital ship. His family employed the likes of Permella in their stately mansion near Lake Wendouree in Ballarat. She knew from the newspapers that Colonel Elliott also had an ankle injury like her Billy.

Permella did not know that the Allies had 12 000 hospital beds ready in Egypt, with more than 50 temporary hospital ships on stand-by. Everyone had expected the evacuation to be a bloodbath—but it was not so. With so few casualties, the Colonel and Billy got the best of treatment. But there was no need for officers to rough it with the 'other ranks'. Colonel Elliott went off to the No. 1 General Hospital at the Heliopolis Palace, while Private Sinnett was sent to the 3rd Auxiliary Hospital at the Cairo Sporting Club. He was delighted to find himself sharing a ward with his pals, Hughie Kelly and George Smith. They also shared an old joke: the No. 1 Hospital was a nut house because it had a colonel. Pompey Elliott was back on duty in half the time it took Billy, which seems to confirm Billy's injury was a gunshot wound rather than a sprain.

In Egypt, the brass—with time on their hands—worried about men in the ranks with time on their hands. They issued a constant flow of orders. Gambling was forbidden. Men should not become 'familiar with the natives'. Soldiers must stop taking possession of compartments in carriages set apart for females because it was 'preventing veiled ladies from traveling'. Men must take greater care with hygiene.

Billy wouldn't have been the only one to scratch his head with this order:

> *Soldiers suffering from venereal disease are to report themselves without delay; all hair must be cut short; all natives found defecating or micturating will be handed over to the Native Police for punishment. Officers Commanding Mounted Brigade will instruct their Sanitary Squads to see that the Natives' Latrines are carefully disinfected; horse manure from the lines of the 7th Regt. must in future be put in a heap on the far side of the ditch running behind the men's mess room...; it has become the custom for soldiers to pass urine in other places than in latrine buckets and urinals. This is a filthy practice and men doing so will be crimed...*(AIF Routine Daily Orders 1915-16).

Billy was surprised by a visit from his brother Samuel—or Henry, as he now insisted on being called for reasons that were nobody's business but his own. He had enlisted on 2 July 1915, weeks before Billy, but his attestation document wasn't completed until late October when almost immediately promoted to corporal. He had not arrived in Egypt until 7 December 1915—at a time when there was no point sending new soldiers to Gallipoli. Henry explained that he had been assigned to the Army Medical Corps (AMC), and held back until the numbers of casualties became critical. He embarked from Melbourne on the *Ascanius* on 10 November in charge of five privates, members of the AMC. They were all young unmarried men on 6 shillings a day. As their leader, Corporal Sinnett was on 9 shillings, but allotted 6/6 to his wife, Annie May. She was not to benefit from that income for very long.

There is no record of the conversation between the

brothers, but it is not hard to imagine the line it took. A lot had happened at home in the five months that Billy had been away, and he was anxious for Samuel/Henry to fill him in. He was impatient to hear the news about Permella and their new baby, but Henry reminded him that he'd sailed before the birth. He confirmed that Permella had moved in with Connie, and the tongues had been wagging around Ballarat. The gossips were swapping guesses about the father of Connie's latest baby, Mavis.

Billy wanted news of their other sisters, Minnie and Lilly. Henry had no encouraging news about Minnie. After two girls, her baby boy, Bertie, didn't seem to have brought Minnie and Herbert any closer together. Herbert Allen never fully trusted Minnie after her affair with Crago way back when she was a flibbertigibbet. Herbert joined up in August, but he refused to put Minnie down as his next-of-kin—giving his father's name instead. What was Minnie supposed to live on with four kids? Three of them were his. He should've looked after them at least. Anyway, Herbert was discharged on medical grounds, the lucky bastard. He kept getting bad ear infections. He was now back with Minnie and all the kids.

What about Lilly, then? At least one of the Sinnett marriages was a goer. The last Henry had heard was that little Willie Coombes was walking and saying a few words, but he too was a sickly child. Maybe Henry was still brooding about his own son, Charlie, who died in Bacchus Marsh three years ago that month. Just seven months on this earth, poor little feller.

Young Syd? Silly bugger can't wait to join up. Dad won't give his consent. But Mum would be happy to see another one of her boys getting knocked around for King and Country. Syd asked his parents to put his age up to 18, like Harry Matheson had. But a blind man would see Syd was a mere stripling at 17. He was in a good job as a butcher. Best off doing the butchering at home.

Billy recalled how Henry, Syd and he himself had talked about the war a year ago. They had been stupid. Here, you stick your head up and a sniper gets a crack at you. It's not man-to-man like at home. It's legalised murder. Futile. After all those months, all our dead men, what do we do? Give the Turks back the land we won.

The brothers did not meet again in Egypt. Henry was admitted to the 1st Australian Defence Hospital at Abbassieh on 8 March with synovitis of the knee. Rheumatism had flared up. Bill paid a visit but was told that he'd been transferred to No 4 Auxiliary Hospital. He made a dash for No 4, only to find that Henry had been moved to No 1 General Hospital. Without warning, time was up. He had to dash back to re-join his battalion—not able to say even a token goodbye. Bill didn't know that Henry would soon be going home to Australia. Indeed, there were lots of things Bill didn't know about his big brother—yet. The doctors decided Henry needed 'three months change' and he sailed on the *Kanowna* for Melbourne in May 1916. The 'three months change' turned into a full discharge in February 1917. The brothers wouldn't see each other again for more than three years.

Billy had come of age in the trenches at Gallipoli. It was time to rid himself of his juvenile tag. If Sam could become Henry at the drop of a hat, then Billy would be known from now on as just plain Bill Sinnett.

Bill was eventually back in training. Long marches through the sand hills, drills that clogged up your rifle with sand, digging trenches in the sand and filling them in again. He found himself taking orders from a young sergeant two years younger than him, newly arrived from Melbourne. The clipped, polished tone led Bill to think Sergeant Andrew Kerr was an Englishman. In fact, he'd been born in Melbourne, but he'd been a boarder at the Tonbridge School in Kent. Kerr had just arrived in Egypt with reinforcements for the 22nd Battalion. But under the reorganisation, he was transferred out of the 22nd, and Bill didn't see him again.

Within a week of transferring to the Western Front in July 1916, Andrew Kerr was killed in action. After the war, his wealthy family bought a mansion in Mornington and decided to use it for 'homeless and destitute children'. The Governor-General, Lord Forster, opened the Andrew Kerr Memorial Home in October 1921 (*Argus* 1/10/1921: 8). It would never have crossed Bill Sinnett's mind that his grandchildren would one day be sent to Sergeant Kerr's orphanage during a war that was yet to come.

Once the move to France was decided on, it was rapid. On 18 March, the men were bundled on the train for Alexandria—officers in covered carriages, other ranks in open trucks. For only the second time in seven years, it rained. Arriving in Alexandria wet to the skin, they were rushed aboard the troopship *Llandovery Castle* and sailed for France the next day.

The train that would take the battalion to the front was not due to leave until the following afternoon—time enough for a quick look around this land of frogs and snails, the men reckoned. They deserved it, after all their hard work in the hot Egyptian sun. Fearing a drunken spree, Colonel Smith refused all shore leave. Men became sullen. Bill was sluggish in obeying a routine order. The boss docked him a month's pay. The next day, the battalion disembarked for transfer to the Western Front. Bill's next address was: '22nd Battalion, Somewhere in France'.

Permella wished she too could live 'Somewhere in France'. It'd be better than life with her mother in Ripon Street. She wondered whether Billy ever stopped to think how isolated and confused she was.

10

Slaughterhouse

Accounts of Bill Sinnett's life on the Western Front are second-hand. I can find nothing written by him. There is, however, a vast amount of personal information in his detailed AIF dossier. There are also dossiers of others who fought with him, together with the official daily diaries of his battalion, the history of the battalion, and numerous published histories of the Somme and many personal accounts written by soldiers like Bill. From these sources I have recreated the events that help explain the further changes that occurred in his view of the war and—more importantly for his wife and daughter, the profound changes that he would bring home with him.

In the twenty-first century, the journey from Marseilles in the south to Armentières in the north takes less than six hours by train. In March 1916, the troop train took nearly three days. As it wound its way north through the lush vineyards, green meadows, and yellow and pink spring blossoms of the sun-blest Rhone Valley, the heat of Egypt was quickly forgotten. The skies turned grey and light rain began to fall. At Aire at 2 o'clock in the morning of 29 March, it was snowing.

A long march over dirty cobblestones finally took the 22nd Battalion to Fleurbaix, near Armentières. Many men had swollen and blistered feet, but they were more concerned by the thumping of distant artillery, and in the night sky, the flash of the big guns and flares. When the Battalion moved into the shallow, damaged breastworks, however, there was nothing more than sniping and occasional shelling by the Germans. For more than a month, they engaged in more training, long marches, laying cables, repairing wiring, and digging defences. They suffered only minor casualties, with random shelling and an occasional bomb accident. Little wonder they called this area the nursery—it provided a gentle introduction to war on the Western Front. Bill Sinnett probably thought trench life in May and June of 1916 was a breeze compared with the cruel hills of Gallipoli. Men moved without hindrance through communication trenches winding through flat green fields and hedgerows. Food was varied and came up every night on a tramway, and water was laid on through pipes.

However, a new phase of the war was about to start, and Bill would soon learn the differences between trench warfare at Gallipoli and trench warfare on the Western Front. By July, they were engaged in a bloody, destructive conflict that made Gallipoli look like just a warm-up bout.

Even hardened eyewitnesses, like the officer who wrote the history of the 22nd Battalion, struggled with the horrifying truth: 'It is not easy to write the story of Pozières, the bloodiest and most costly battle in which the Battalion was ever engaged.' (Gorman 1919: 32). Yet, it was the Australian Army's first success since Gallipoli's Lone Pine.

Like most people at home in 1916, Permella knew nothing about Pozières, except the carefully managed versions in the newspapers. I visited Pozières on the trail of my grandfather in 2006, 90 years on, and found an unremarkable village on an old ramrod-straight Roman road between Albert and Bapaume. In 1916, it was home to not more than 300 souls. This small village, I learnt, sat on a strategic ridge, giving the Germans control of a strong artillery position. If the Allies could take Pozières, they could take Thiepval, another German stronghold, and push on from there.

In July 1916, entrenched machine guns and heavy artillery were too much for the British who had made four attacks and failed. A new plan would have the Australian infantry attack up a slope in the face of these German machine guns and artillery on the high ground. Having walked the area and read numerous accounts of the Australian battle at Pozières, I still can't get my head around how the commanders could expect ordinary men to run across no-man's-land towards these murderous machine guns, each firing off more than 500 rounds a minute. Hundreds of men would die without making it halfway across.

Yet somehow, on 23 July, the Australians managed to take the Pozières trench and capture a seemingly impenetrable German bunker known as 'Gibraltar' which had been the only structure in the area to withstand the fierce artillery bombardment (Bean 1929 Vol. 3: 455). By the morning of 24 July, the Australians had taken Pozières completely and pushed the line forward 1 000 metres. However, the Germans counter-attacked with deadly shelling and machine gun fire at their flank. Under relentless pounding for three days and nights, the shallow Australian trenches were blown apart. Men sheltering in shell holes were blown to pieces.

On 27 July, fresh Australian troops, including Bill's battalion, moved in to take over. By now Bill had almost a year's experience and was seen as a veteran, but it was easy to forget he had never taken part in a major battle before. What did he think when the surviving men from the 6th Battalion shuffled past, exhausted? Eyewitnesses wrote of haggard faces bowed down, not looking newcomers in the eye as they passed. Their success in taking the village of Pozières had come at a terrible price. In just a few days, the Australians had lost 5 285 men. But, unlike the disastrous defeat at Fromelles—which had cost just as many casualties—at least they had something to show for it. It was now up to the new men to hold their gains.

The Germans had the fresh men under observation until they reached the trenches just beyond the village, and gave them no time to settle in. Their big guns pounded the Australians mercilessly. The high explosive shells were ferocious. Piles of Australian ammunition exploded. The noise was deafening. Telephone lines were cut and couldn't be repaired. At times smoke made it impossible to see. The Australian trenches were like a massive abattoir. Bodies lay on the firesteps and duckboards, in the saps and the crosspoints. I think Bill Sinnett would never get these images out of his head. Stretcher-bearers splashed with blood, and exhausted, carrying out hundreds of men, some dead, some dying, some who might live but with limbs missing.

For three days and three nights, non-stop, high explosives smashed the trenches, rendering no-man's-land a chaotic wasteland of hundreds of primeval craters. Fragments ricocheted randomly. Dark, stinking smoke got into the mouth and nostrils. A shell burst 30 yards dead ahead, the flash stabbing the eye like broken glass. The stench of death fouled the air. Men on both sides lay still unburied from the week before. It was near impossible to clear out the wounded. All you could do was try to ride it out—lie prone, crouch low, stand at your peril.

Three nights without a decent sleep, Bill curled up in his possie, trembling. Without warning, he felt the weight of sandbags and earth crushing down on him against his waist.

Then higher. He couldn't scream out, the dirt squashed his lips tight, crushing his torso like a bag of straw. He could see nothing. For a time, he lost reality under the black, damp earth. One arm free. Someone gripped his wrist. A man called him. A hand on Bill's wrist tugging him. Other men digging. The sandbags moved. His head was free. And his torso. It's OK, cobber. We've got you. Pull yourself up now. There's other men buried. The voice dashed off, leaving Bill to clear the dirt out of his mouth and ears as best he could, without water.

He scrambled to help others. He had to walk over dead men to get to men half-buried, crying out in pain and fear. Dozens of men of the 22nd were buried dead or alive. Some got out, like Bill, while they were still breathing. On their feet in no time, no harm done, some would brag later. Dusted off, given a swig of rum, and sent back to fight again. Expected to get over it like you would a bout of the shits.

The relentless German bombardment and gas bombs kept the men in a constant state of terror. There was no let up. No one slept. On the third day, the 22nd Battalion was to be relieved by the 21st. They started to move in late at night, but the German bombardment lifted to yet another level, so intense that no one could move until daylight on the fourth day. During the night, reinforcements from the 21st got lost in the thick fog. The bombardments had changed the shape and outline of the trenches. Only when the 21st finally took over could the 22nd count its dead, attend to the wounded and praise the survivors. It's a great job, this: if you don't win the raffle today, you get another ticket tomorrow.

On the night of 4 August, the 22nd moved to the front line again. The men were sick of playing sitting ducks. This time they were going over the top. The sergeant prepared his section. You have to cross 500 yards of no-man's-land before you reach the German trenches. When you get the word, you get up and run like buggery. If a man cops one near you and falls—and half of you will—don't stop.

At 1730 hours, they moved to the forward trenches, platoon by platoon, at two-minute intervals. Under heavy bombardment, casualties were already severe. One man in every four or five did not make it to the attack, but the rest pressed on. By 1930 hours, all seemed to be in readiness for the attack, except that the night sky was too light. More delay. More jangling nerves. At 2115 hours, the Australian artillery started a barrage that would soften up the enemy. Music to their ears. But it stopped as suddenly as it started. Minute Waltz. They had given them a seven-hour barrage before, which meant plenty of warning and time to prepare their defences. The brevity this time was designed to confuse the Germans.

Fix bayonets and prepare to make the assault: an officer's voice startled them. The sharp clicking of steel. A last puff on a fag. Remember, boys, no retreat and no prisoners.

They were just out of their trenches when dozens of dazzling flares lit up the sky, red, green, white. The Germans were ready for them, make no mistake. Rabbits caught in the lights. When the machine guns opened fire, many men didn't last more than a few steps.

When the flares burned out, came the flashing and clattering of a thousand guns, shells and shrapnel. Bill jack-knifed from a red-hot jab in his chest, fell to the ground, stunned. Instinct told him to crawl out of the line of fire. He slumped into a shell crater. Blood seeped from his right thigh. He was not alone in the crater. One man lay with his eyes locked open. Bill crawled over and shut them, took his water bottle, and sank even lower. Two more bodies in the crater, mangled and re-mangled, buried and unburied.

Hours later, two men kicked him softly and found he was alive. They stretchered him to a dressing-station, then trolleyed him to a field ambulance, miles behind the line. The Casualty Clearing Station quickly triaged the latest arrivals. Those who would probably recover with the least treatment were dealt with on the spot. They would be sped back to the front. For the rest, there were simply too many casualties and too few doctors. The nurses, and orderlies did what they could for the hopeless. Orderlies arranged the burials. The seriously wounded were cleared to the base hospitals.

Bill was taken by motor ambulance to No. 10 General Hospital at Rouen. The hospital was just another battlefield. Soldiers covered in blood and mud lay on stretchers lining the middle of the giant tents. Doctors and nurses struggled to move between beds. They ignored the moans and groans of those who merely had a broken leg or shrapnel in their buttocks. No names. No time for personal niceties. One doctor measured his patients by classifications: last night he had done seven abdomens, six transfusions, and three amputations. A young nurse darted in a frenzy from one wrecked body to another. Too many men were equally urgent.

Bill would not yet know the worst of the battle he had just taken part in. The battalion had commissioned eleven new lieutenants just before their attack on Pozières. Within two days, six of these men had been killed and three wounded. Between 27 July and 8 August, Bill's battalion lost 33 officers and 763 men (Gorman 1919: 32–34). Overall, at Fromelles and Pozières in just seven weeks, the AIF had suffered 23 000 casualties—more than in the entire eight-month campaign at Gallipoli. For that, they had gained a few hundred yards of land and a village now reduced to rubble and brick dust.

For the widows and orphans of husbands and fathers buried in the tiny village of Pozières and their descendants, this battle remains a monument to the lunacy of war. For the wives and children whose husbands and fathers came home with the madness of Pozières in their souls, it was just the start of another story.

11

Patched up

Bill Sinnett lay in the queue for more than a day before a doctor finally had time to look at him. Patches of blood had seeped from the shrapnel wounds. His chest burned. He was surprised to be reminded that he had been shot in the leg, too. He ached all over. The doctor was blunt. Not bad enough to get a wooden cross. Bad enough for a Blighty as soon as there's a spot on a boat. You're a lucky beggar. A few scraps of metal in the chest, a bullet in the leg—small price to get you out of that hellhole.

A trip to the old Blighty meant Bill would be out of the front line for a while. Had he been worse—not likely to be fit within six months—he would have been sent back to Australia. What he would have given to be sent home for his recovery, if only for a few months. Instead, after three days of superficial cleaning and dressing of the wounds, he was put on the hospital ship *Marama* at Le Havre. An orderly pinned a label on his tunic indicating his destination in England—the Cambridge Military Hospital at Aldershot, Hampshire.

Bill's injuries would soon heal. The visible scars would fade in time, but his apprehension was more deep-rooted. In the trenches, everyone dealt with fear in a different way. Bill had seen how some men sucked at a cold cigarette, or shuffled a deck of cards, sang a hymn, had yet another piss before their officer put the whistle to his mouth. He had seen men go to pieces when they saw a mate killed. He had seen others—with nothing to prove, or everything to prove—volunteer for acts of stupefying courage, or mindless folly. The nurses supposed every soldier had feelings of both cowardice and courage on the battlefield. 'Courage is nothing more than hiding your fear,' one said. 'Some disguise it better—and get the medals.' She had treated men who received bravery awards, and most were reluctant to talk about what they had done to earn them. Recognition was random. In every battle, the nameless killed the faceless in the dark. Countless acts of bravery went unrecognised and unreported—and so did countless moments of fear.

On 31 August 1916, more than three weeks after her husband's brush with death, Permella stood pale and immobile, her baby (my mother) crying on one arm, a cable in the other hand. Her mother, Catherine, read the cable. Then the meaning hit: 'No details of the wounds are known...nor the hospital but assumed not to be serious wound.' Permella laughed with relief, again, as she had after Gallipoli when it was only an ankle. She did not consider herself superstitious, but she wondered if the next cable, the third, would be the last.

By the time Permella read that news, Bill was already walking again, with the aid of a stick, and venturing out a little more each day. The clean sheets, the fresh air, and the sense of orderliness bucked him up, as it had in Egypt. The food was even better—sliced bread and fried bacon for breakfast, Irish stew for dinner, served hot, and with a smile to match. Soon he and a few others were allowed to go out of the hospital every other day. The doctors and nurses had enough to do without convalescents cluttering up the wards.

Back at the hospital, a new topic of conversation was raging—as it was at home. Australia had initially promised just 20 000 men, but by this time, a quarter of a million volunteers had been sent to the front; a further 50 000 were in training awaiting transport, and others were on troopships steaming to the front (*Argus* 19/8/1916: 18). But the rapacious beast of war consumed more than 26 000 casualties at Gallipoli and another 28 000 at Fromelles and Pozières. A referendum on conscription—strictly speaking, a plebiscite—was to be held in Australia on 28 October. Soldiers would get a vote, too, if they were over 21. Like many other soldiers, Bill had never voted in any election before. The issue was dividing the soldiers—volunteers all of them—just as it was dividing families and communities back home.

Bill's young brother, Syd, reckoned if he was old enough to fight for King and Empire, he was old enough to vote. He'd enlisted in July, aged 18, and was on the troopship *Nestor* en route to London with the 8th Battalion, due to disembark in mid-November. The *Argus* reckoned a young soldier like him '… will vote more intelligently than will the shirker of 21 years and over …' (*Argus* 8/9/1916: 6). Bill had fought alongside young men like Syd. German guns didn't care whether an enemy was 18 or 38. Some of them would never vote, any time. Some units were desperately below strength, and the survivors were exhausted. Hadn't the 1914 and 1915 men, like Bill, done their share? Or would he be on the other side of the debate? Could he rely for his life on a man who didn't want to be alongside him in the trenches? Wouldn't it be better to have a man who had put his hand up willingly, if a little late? How could he wish the horror of war on other young men?

Two days before the rolls closed for the referendum, Bill Sinnett was discharged from the Aldershot hospital. His injuries had required 37 days in care. Never-ending intakes of new casualties caused doctors to be sparing with their paperwork. His discharge report stated simply: 'G.S.W. chest. Injury slight...Superficial wounds. No injury to ribs. Metal removed. Result complete recovery with no defect.' There was no reference to the wounds to his leg. Nothing about being buried alive in the trenches. Psychological wounds were none of a doctor's business.

He was granted extra leave but had to report for regular medical checks. He paid the mandatory visit to AIF Headquarters (HQ) at Horseferry Road in Westminster. The soldiers called it Cowpunt Road, just as they called redheads 'Bluey'. He collected his pay and a new uniform, confirmed arrangements for his medical supervision, and enrolled to vote. I visited Horseferry Road recently. Within sight and sound of Big Ben, this now-salubrious precinct of London was then 'a reeking slum with half a dozen second-rate public houses within a stone's throw and Delilah lurking up every murky passage' (*British Australasian*, 22/2/1917). *The Times* of London worried about these innocent Australians abroad:

> *It is cruel recompense to men who have come halfway round the globe to fight England's battles that they should be allowed, innocently and unforwarned to run the risk of being robbed by these birds of prey of all they possess.* (*Times*, 9/7/1915)

Warnings about female birds of prey were gilt-edged invitations to some Australian soldiers—and their officers. On brief respite from the daily threat of death, starved of the company of women and free from the shackles of home, some men were more than willing to rendezvous with Delilah up a murky passage. After months in the filth and squalor of the trenches, the seedy hotels free-flowing with alcohol were 5-star deluxe.

Permella wouldn't have liked to think about it, but these innocents abroad, cashed-up compared to their British counterparts, took great pleasure in their leisure in Blighty. Thousands of them contracted the 'disease of leave' (Butler, 1940). Matters became so dire that 'Blue Light' rooms were set up at HQ where men could seek confidential treatment any hour day and night. All men arriving in London were handed a card saying: 'No Names, Regimental Numbers or questions regarding identity will be asked.' But social niceties were maintained—there were separate rooms for officers and other ranks. The preventive measures didn't work. By the end of the war, at least 55 000 Australian soldiers had been treated for VD—not far short of the overall numbers who were killed in the War (Stanley 2010: 228). Many soldiers were reckless: they knew the serious risk to their health, but weighed that risk against the 'punishment' of being sent back to Australia. Back home, a single man might be excused for paying the price of sowing some wild oats: 'boys will be boys'. A married man had more to explain, and many a wife refused to accept infidelity. Divorce rates escalated after the war. In 1911, there were 99 divorces per 100 000 couples in the State of Victoria; this rose to 145 in 1919 and 168 in 1929 (Victorian Year Books for respective years). The press carried reports of returned soldiers taking up an inordinate amount of the courts' time (*Argus* 22/11/1919: 6; 17/7/1919: 7; 13/11/1919: 9).

Married men were warned to get out of the Horseferry Road area quick smart. Did Bill stay away, or did he lose more than his Kodak in the war? His dossier makes no mention of VD; but on a number of occasions, he sent cables home to Permella asking her to send money. Perhaps he was a heavy gambler, or drank a lot, or was careless with his wallet. We'll never know.

The Australian Red Cross found Bill a room at 6 shillings a week at the Union Jack Club, near enough for his regular medical check-ups. He was able to get free meals at the nearby Anzac Buffet served by Australian women resident in London who were, presumably, a cut above the local birds of prey.

There are some uncanny parallels between Bill Sinnett's few precious weeks in London in 1916 and my own in 1953. London became the centre of the universe for him as it would for me, his grandson, fresh out of my war at the Ballarat Orphanage decades later. Like me, my grandfather would have found London a wonderland. He would have haunted the amazing Underground, getting off to gawp at the shops in Regent Street; or alighting at Piccadilly Circus, strolling to Trafalgar Square to gaze up at the grand monument of Nelson. He would have walked, as I did, to St Paul's Cathedral and on to the Tower of London, watching the hydraulic motors lifting up the roadway to let steamers pass. He would have crossed the Thames at Westminster Bridge, ambled past the Houses of Parliament and Big Ben, and on to Westminster Abbey in the fading light. On a weekend, like me, he might have strolled through the great park to Buckingham Palace, stopping a while to listen to the orators at Hyde Park corner and perhaps joining in the heckling and repartee. At night, he could attend free concerts two or three times a week and see moving pictures—just as I could marvel at the wondrous novelty of television at the start of another era. A man and his grandson could never tire of London. It restored our souls after the punishing time we wanted to put behind us.

At the AIF command depot on the edge of the Salisbury Plain, he passed more fitness tests and was deemed ready for another stint. After revelling in the peaceful English autumn with endless calm blue skies, its gentle greens, creamy yellows, and warm russets, he would soon return to the drab skies of France and its gluey mud, black filth, and the stench of death.

He had one last duty in London. On 28 October he joined the final group of soldiers to answer the conscription question being put to the Australian people at home that very day. Some troops at the front had already voted in advance of the official date. Ballot papers completed by the troops were sent to London and the results were cabled immediately (*Argus* 2/9/1916: 18). Prime Minister Hughes had predicted a resounding 'Yes' vote from the soldiers, and the result would send a compelling message to the people at home that the troops wanted help. However, Hughes was embarrassed by the soldiers' ballot returns which were indecisive at best. There was no political capital in them.

How individual units of the AIF voted was never disclosed (Robson, 1970: 107). There was also a curious silence in official records from the front. The daily diary of the 22nd Battalion did not mentioned the plebiscite, nor did its battalion history. We can never know which way Bill Sinnett or his pals voted.

When Bill Sinnett began his journey back to his unit on the Western Front on 11 November 1916, the war had precisely two more years to run. No one knew it then. Away from the front line for more than four months, his body had repaired, but there was a persistent tight knot in his guts. It wasn't just the fear of the shelling, and living like an animal in the trenches. He dreaded being told about the men he would not meet again. He would now have to confront the friends of the many men who had been killed in his absence. Only fragments of news had filtered through while he was in hospital. He had seen a few lists at Horseferry Road.

Although he'd been passed as fully fit and re-trained in England, he was subjected to ten more days training at Etaples in France. It was an astonishing place. Before the war it was a modest fishing town and port at the mouth of the River Canche. Now it was a massive Army Base Camp, the largest ever set up by the British overseas. It could accommodate over 100 000 military personnel serving in the training camp, supply depot, detention centre for prisoners, and medical hub, with up to twenty hospitals capable of accommodating 22 000 casualties. A network of railways, canals, and roads connected the camp to the southern and eastern battlefronts. Ships arrived every day carrying troops, supplies, guns, and equipment across the Channel.

Etaples was, above all, a brutal place. Sergeant Majors bullied and bludgeoned men in the bull ring with fanatical fitness trials, bayonet-fights, and route marches.

Bill was ordered to re-join his battalion on 24 November. He would not have suspected that he was in for the worst winter in living memory. Out of action since 4 August 1916, Bill reported back for duty at Fricourt on 24 November. He was treated like a long-lost brother. Where had he been all this while? Back home to see the baby? And make a new one too, they'd wager. He wished it were true. Many a soldier had been sent home, including his big brother, Sam. Sore knee, poor bugger! What about a man with a new baby at home? She'd be walking by now. And, chattering, too.

After the handshakes and another tot of rum, Bill wanted to know about the glum news. Some had been killed on the same day that he'd copped his wounds. Others might have been killed that day, too, but men were blown to pieces or buried alive and not declared dead until there was time to check eyewitness accounts. On the same day that Bill was put out of action at Pozières, Bob Smart was reported missing; but it took months before he was confirmed killed in action. Eyewitness Corporal John McLeod reported Bob's last words: 'I don't think I will see Surrey Hills again'.

Bob's brother, George, had been killed in one of the last actions at Gallipoli in December. It was heartbreaking that both brothers should die. But they were not the only ones. Charlie and Roy Bettles had sailed with Bill on the *Anchises*. Charlie was reported wounded on the same day as Bill, but it would take 12 months for a court of inquiry to declare that he had been killed on 29 July. Roy had been killed in action at Pozières a few days earlier. Roy used to tell the story that the AIF had sent a letter to his home in September 1915 declaring him AWL and ordering him to report back to camp or else. At that very time, Roy and Charlie were on board the *Anchises* on their way to the war with Bill Sinnett. If only they had all missed the boat.

All the stories were sad, but the death of Snowy Tait, another Ballarat lad from the *Anchises*, was the most moving for Bill. He knew Snowy well from Skipton Street and had bought clothes from him at Snow's drapery in Sturt Street. Snowy's boss was a good bloke. Hands on heart, he promised to reinstate his workers upon return from the war (*Courier* 15/7/1915). Snowy was in a raiding party when a bomb landed among the Australians. He threw himself on it to save his pals. It was his 20th birthday, and there was a birthday parcel from home. Afterwards, the chaplain opened it and found sweets and a money belt. He shared the sweets around among the men of his section and posted the money and belt back to Snowy's parents with a letter saying how bravely he had died.

Why Snowy, Bob, George? Why Charlie and Roy, but not Bill? He always called 'heads' at two-up, but he knew the pennies had to come up tails eventually. Permella was depressed. She wished he could get a sore knee to bring him home.

Did people at home know what 'Somewhere in France' was like when they addressed their Christmas cards? One man's mother was shocked to learn that men fought on the Sabbath. Another mother couldn't believe that battles continued through teeming rain. If only it was just rain. Men plunged knee-deep in mud, even waist-deep 'somewhere in France'. Horses reared and snorted, sinking up to their shoulders. The mud at Ginchy was so deep and thick it took all a man's strength to walk five steps without stumbling or losing his sodden boots in the gluepot. Bill and his pals had to lie down to sleep in the slush and mud 'somewhere in France'. They pissed and shat in the nearest shell hole, and often the rain didn't wash away the accumulating waste or the persistent stench of dead corpses. 'Somewhere in France' many men now expected never to get home.

'Somewhere in France' Bill and his cobbers feasted on frozen bread and bully-beef for Christmas, eating quickly because fighting could resume at any time. And it did. High Command ordered a continuous artillery barrage throughout Christmas Day. And on New Year's Day 1917, Bill's Battalion's artillery hurled tons of shells at the Germans—a resolution to carry on from last year (Gorman 1919: 48).

The Australian attack on the seemingly impregnable Hindenburg Line at Bullecourt requires no commentary from me, except to say Bill Sinnett's battalion was the hardest hit. In just 24 hours, the 22nd lost 16 officers out of 33 and 422 other ranks out of 842 (Gorman 1919: 60). No matter how you look at these staggering losses, statistics could never express the psychological devastation of those who survived. Men like Bill Sinnett, who fought through this brutality and survived, paid a cost that could never be calculated. Permella might have prayed for a wound that would force her husband to come home. Her man would return to her eventually, but after Pozières and Bullecourt, would he be the man she first loved?

12

Blighty 1917

Bill Sinnett had lost the taste for adventure long ago. Bill's daughter was 18 months old by then, and he wondered constantly what she looked like. If only he could have slipped home for a few weeks.

Just after his 23rd birthday in August 1917, the battalion prepared to move to the battlefields of Ypres just over the border in Belgium. Bill must have been relieved when he was awarded two weeks' leave, from 18 September. He quickly made his way back to London, collected his pay at Cowpunt Road, and made a beeline for the War Chest Fund Dining Room for a three-course dinner. Soldiers could sleep and eat there, and the lounge had writing facilities. A string quartet played during lunch and dinner. Bill found the atmosphere starchy. The YMCA on The Strand had everything a man could want.

Bill found the atmosphere in London had changed. The war had lost its glamour. People everywhere were talking about Lieutenant Siegfried Sassoon's statement to his commanding officer, 'Finished with War: a soldier's declaration'. The statement was read aloud in the House of Commons on 30 July 1917 and published in the *Times* the next day. Soldiers on leave like Bill passed around tattered copies:

> *I have seen and endured the suffering of the troops, and I can no longer be a party to prolong these sufferings for ends which I believe to be evil and unjust. I am not protesting against the conduct of the war, but against the political errors and insincerities for which the fighting men are being sacrificed …*

Sassoon had ceremoniously thrown his Military Cross

into the River Mersey, and refused to return to the front. The authorities were perplexed: how would you make a charge of cowardice stick when the man had been awarded the Military Cross for 'conspicuous gallantry'? Instead, they had him diagnosed with 'shell shock' and referred him to Craiglockhart Hospital in Scotland. Mental illness was the textbook public explanation. Sassoon was out of sight, but certainly not out of mind.

In Hyde Park, Bill could tune in to a speaker shouting above the catcalls and interjections of a noisy and threatening crowd:

> *If kings and lords want to make war, if financiers and manufacturers want to make war, if those competing with one another for wealth and power in the world want to make war, let them and their sons take up arms. [Boos] The workers of Britain have no quarrel with the workers of Germany. Their enemy is not the working class of Germany; the enemy is not the ordinary honest man who is decent and hard-working; the enemy is not the young men on the factory floor or down the mines. [You're the enemy, you traitor.]*
>
> *Thousands of good men lie dead; conscientious and simple men lie dead; brave men in the prime of their lives lie dead...[Blasphemy!] And why, I ask you? In the false name of allegiance to this nation and to the Empire. [Blackguard!] But I tell you, gentlemen, allegiance to the nation is a sham, a perversity, a damnable misrepresentation that sends innocent men to fight a futile battle which is none of their making.* [Boos!]

Bill would have remembered Permella expressing ideas like these two years ago when she was trying to persuade him to stay home. I don't know the precise moment when my grandfather lost the naïve faith that sent him to the war. Gallipoli was bad enough, but how could a man keep the faith after Pozières and Bullecourt?

What he needed above all was peace. Yet, here in the sanctuary of London he found it hard to get a good night's sleep. For weeks on end, he had slept amid ferocious non-stop bombardments of shells, but the noise of the traffic along The Strand disturbed him just as much. He'd been at war now for two years. In a few days, he would be sent back for more. Instead of making the most of his time away from the front, regaining strength, he dreamed each night about the trenches. He felt sick, but the military doctors found no symptoms.

My grandfather's leave expired on the morning of 1 October. Seven days after that date, he was arrested outside the YMCA, carrying a false leave pass. Hauled before a court-martial, he was asked to explain himself. What could he say? Could he have offered an 'I'm-not-the-only-one' defence? After all, more Australian soldiers were court-martialled for being AWL or deserting in October 1917 than in any other month of the war (Carlyon 2006: 510). Would these spit-and-polish officers understand that men had joined up expecting the war would be short and exciting, but found life in the trenches a never-ending black night of torment? Could he tell them about the nightmares that haunted him every night? Could he tell them he was disillusioned, demoralised, exhausted, had stopped thinking about how he and his cobbers were fighting; had started to think about why they were fighting?

He simply pleaded guilty and offered no excuses. He served 28 days in detention on no pay and a forfeit of an extra nine days' pay. This was almost certainly one of those times when he wrote to Permella asking her to send him some money.

He'd been in London from mid-September and his detention ended on 8 November. This period of time coincided with the ferocious 3rd Ypres campaign from Menin Road to Passchendaele. In those eight savage weeks, another 27 791 Australians were killed or wounded. In aerial photographs taken after the battle for Passchendaele, half a million shell holes could be seen in the half square mile around the village. Some 42 000 British and Australian bodies were never recovered because they had been blown to bits, or sank, wounded or exhausted, drowned in deep shell craters filled with glutinous mud (Miller 1993). The very name Passchendaele joined Fromelles, Pozières and Bullecourt as testimonies of the horror, futility, and stupidity of war. In years to come, when people mentioned Passchendaele, Bill Sinnett could never bring himself to say he wasn't there.

13

Tailwind

The exhausted Australian troops were about to withdraw from Passchendaele when Prime Minister Billy Hughes announced another vote on conscription. The first plebiscite, he claimed, had been 'a triumph for the unworthy, the selfish and anti-British in our midst' (*Argus* 13/11/1917: 5). The people had made a grave mistake, he said, and he would give them a chance to redeem themselves. He framed the question for a better result: 'Are you in favour of the proposal of the Commonwealth Government for reinforcing the Commonwealth Forces overseas?' The Australian people would vote five days before the Christmas of 1917.

Hughes had calculated the political risks. He could not afford to upset mothers and wives. Boys aged 18 and 19 would be exempted from military service, and so would all married men. The only men who would be conscripted, he finally announced, would be single men aged between 20 and 44.

Permella was contemptuous, and expected thousands of other wives of serving men would feel the same. Their husbands had already volunteered and were dead, or in mortal danger. When Hughes spoke of conscription, he never mentioned widows and orphans, death or loss. He spoke of women as mothers to the nation and empire. But Permella was not a mother to the nation or the empire. She was mother to Hilda, who had never met her father. And maybe never would. Permella's exclusion from family circles around the plebiscite and other issues worsened her anxiety and loneliness. Birthdays—hers, her husband's, and now her daughter's—fed her gnawing sense of a life unfulfilled. She ached for the warmth and strength of a male body close to hers at night.

Australian troops were to vote on 11 December 1917. I doubt my grandfather wanted to share a trench with someone whose heart wasn't in it. I doubt he thought any man should be compelled to put up with the conditions he'd endured. I doubt he wanted any to live like an animal month in month out. Worlds apart—and perhaps for the last time—Bill and Permella were probably of like mind.

When Bill returned to his battalion at Selles in northeast France late in February 1918, his friends spoke of Passchendaele in muted tones. More men from the *Anchises* had copped it at Passchendaele. Bill James and John Lowerey were gone. Bill remembered they were wounded at Gallipoli, as he was; and all three had been hit again at Pozières. Passchendaele was the third strike for the other two. If Bill Sinnett hadn't been missing in action in London ... In the intimacy of the trenches, your life depended on someone else taking your place on the death list. You never knew from one day to the next which friend crouching beside you was going to cop one. My grandfather's absence raised the stakes for some other man, a Bill James or a John Lowerey. He knew the odds of survival were shortening. Only a minority of the men now were the originals from 1914. He had arrived with the Battalion's 3rd reinforcements in 1915. By Passchendaele in 1917, the battalion had needed 20 sets of reinforcement to replace the dead, wounded, or ill—a complete turnover of men once a year (Gorman 1919: v).

Bill Sinnett knew there were many ways for a malingerer to squib it. Techniques passed quietly among the men. Add egg-white to urine to display signs of kidney disease. Chew cordite to cause an irregular heartbeat. Ingest picric acid (used in explosives) to feign jaundice. Spill half a dozen drops of iodine on tobacco before you smoke to give you a bad heart and a high temperature. Visit a brothel and catch the pox to be sent home. Shoot yourself in the hand or leg to be out of action for months, if not for the duration (Stanley 2010: 66-69). To his credit, my grandfather did not come at any of these. Determined to put his AWL behind him, he would not to be remembered as a shirker.

On 21 March 1918, the Germans launched a massive offensive, employing the greatest artillery barrage ever seen—around 6 000 guns. They surged on a 40-mile front from Arras to St Quentin, and by the end of the month, they had advanced 50 miles, regained almost all the territory lost to the Allies in 1916 and 1917, and captured 90 000 prisoners and 1 000 guns. At that rate, they would be in Paris in a week.

In the first week of April, my grandfather's battalion took over a section of the front near Albert, expecting a massive German assault any day. The days of trench deadlock were over. The Germans had discarded their system of deep defensive trenches in favour of thick-walled concrete pillboxes manned with deadly machine guns defending no-man's-land. The Allies were using creeping barrages: advancing in short bursts behind a progressive artillery bombardment. Australian units were also using bush tactics of nightly raids on German outposts, capturing pockets of prisoners, weapons, and supplies. My grandfather would have found this style of fighting much more to his liking.

On 19 May, his battalion and others attacked the Germans at Ville-sur-Ancre. Under an intense creeping barrage, the infantry advanced to within yards of the enemy and took them by surprise. After hours of heavy hand-to-hand fighting, they captured 330 prisoners and 45 German machine guns. It was the first strategically important village to be won back by the Allies after the German offensive.

At Gallipoli, the senseless waste of life had shocked Bill Sinnett. Now, death had lost its sting. He had seen too many deaths, some accidental, some heroic, some up close and many *en masse*. When Permella sent news that his grandmother, Eliza Stokes, had died in Ballarat on 26 May 1918, Bill didn't weep. Why would he be touched by the death of an 84-year-old far away when he saw good young men dying every day? Besides, his loyalty lay with his father, Edward Sinnett, who had no great affection for his mother Eliza who had put him in prison when he was just a little boy.

Towards the end of June 1918, as the depleted battalion moved to the Villers-Bretonneux area, Bill was transferred into HQ Company. There removed from the worst risks, he could see for himself the state of German prisoners, many very young and inexperienced, all of them fatigued and hungry, demoralised by recent defeats and hit hard by a virulent influenza epidemic. Yet, as Bill marked his 24th birthday in August, Australian losses continued to be high. In one attack at Herleville on 18 August, two-thirds of the men were killed, wounded, or missing. At this low point, the battalion could muster only 70 fighting men (Gorman 1919: 104). It was now the weakest battalion in the 6th Brigade and had to be rested again. By the time the 22nd Battalion was called to the front line again, on 3 October, the so-called invincible Hindenburg line had been smashed and the Australians began to smell victory.

When the battalion attacked the German defences at Beaurevoir and Montbrehain on the night of the 5-6 October, the Australians handed over their strong position to an American unit. That was the end of the war for the 22nd Battalion. On 8 October, Bill went on leave to England for the third time. I suspect this leave was granted on compassionate grounds. There was alarming news from home that weighed heavily on his mind.

When he returned three weeks later, the Germans were all but defeated, and on 11 November, the guns finally fell silent. The battalion's historian claimed the troops accepted the news with 'singular calm' (Gorman 1919: 116). I can't imagine that Bill Sinnett greeted the news that had just come from home with singular calm.

PART 4
THE HOME FRONT

On her husband's return she had to learn again to be submissive, to leave things in his hands ... She had to learn to tolerate his new friends and to accept that there was a part of his life which she could not share. In the early days of his demobilisation especially, but often for much longer, she had to be his emotional support as he struggled to cope again with domestic and civilian life ... Such strains proved too much for many marriages.

—Michael McKernan, 1980

14

Going home

When I was a 'neglected child' from the Ballarat Orphanage and visited my grandmother's melancholic house, I formed a strong impression that she was protecting some dark secrets about my mother—who was missing in action. It never occurred to me at the time that Permella had dark secrets of her own—that she was protecting herself as well as my grandfather and my mother. Secrets she took to the grave are not now as safe as she believed. Just as my grandfather's military history was well documented and archived for future readers, some of Permella's secrets can be found in the public arena, in records in the archives and in muted family stories.

During the last months of the war in 1918, when my mother was not yet three years old, Permella and Auntie Connie were twin targets of unpleasant gossip around the neighbourhood. Their babies were due in November of 1918, and it was impossible any longer to conceal their condition. Permella's baby girl arrived first, two days before the armistice. It is possible she went to Melbourne and used a false name for the infant. I can find no birth registered in Ballarat but a baby registered as Jean Thelma Adams, was born in Collingwood. The baby's surname is Permella's maiden name, but the birth certificate supplies no surname for the mother or father, and the mother's given name is not given as Permella. It was common practice at the time for mothers to be shielded from the shame of an irregular pregnancy. In later official records, the baby was simply named Jean Adams.

Connie's baby boy arrived two days later, with military

precision on Armistice Day. She named him George Douglas Peace Matheson. This was Connie's second ex-nuptial child. The second she confessed to. She had dealt with her husband's outrage before.

Although the letters have not survived, I know from court records and newspaper reports that both expectant mothers had written to their husbands overseas to break the news. It's likely that they decided to write at the same time, but I have every reason to think the two letters would have been utterly unalike. Connie's letter to her husband would have been blunt. She had long stopped caring what Harry Matheson thought. When pressed, Connie didn't bother to conceal her lover's name. Charles Lees had skipped town, anyway, the rogue. Why should she protect him now?

Harry Matheson was recovering in England from a self-inflicted wound that relieved him from the trenches when he received the startling news in August 1918. He was furious. He swore Connie would pay for her treachery. He wrote to his brother, John, in Ballarat to tell him that he was going to London the next day to start a 'Divorce Suite' (sic). He would cut off her military allotment at once and asked his brother to act on his behalf in that matter. John Matheson had sailed to the war (on the same ship as Bill Sinnett) back in August 1915, but was sent home early in 1917 (also with a self-inflicted wound). John Matheson contacted the AIF in Australia twice, demanding they stop paying Connie. They wouldn't act. They needed Harry's written authority.

Harry Matheson was among the first soldiers to arrive home, reaching Melbourne on New Year's Day 1919. He was spoiling for a fight. As he had done in the past, he raced home to Ballarat in a white-hot rage. Yet, for all his indignation, it became clear in the months that followed that

Harry Matheson had already met another woman. Perhaps he was nobody's fool after all.

Harry's rage, confected or not, sadly counted for nothing in the end. After just three months, baby George Douglas Peace Matheson died on 10 February 1919 from gastroenteritis. Connie had lost three babies now. In addition to George and Mavis Matheson, she had also lost Francis Charles Sinnett in January 1918. Francis was cryptically described as 'by adoption known as Nelson' but was buried under the name Matheson. Harry had seemed genuinely to be moved by the death in 1916 of baby Mavis, but with the births and deaths of Mavis, George and Francis Sinnett—possibly none were his—he was beyond sympathy for Connie.

When Harry made a direct request, the Army ceased making payments to Connie from March 1919. After that, although estranged and headed for divorce, she continued to be entitled to a pension of 17/6 a week because she was still the wife of the incapacitated Harry Matheson—if only for a short time more.

And Permella's letter to Bill? I can't imagine what words she used to break the news. Judging by the events in their relationship over the next few years, my belief is that Permella would not have hit her husband between the eyes with the cold facts in the same style as Connie. I prefer to envisage a long, thoughtfully crafted letter. She'd been an utter fool. She'd let down the man she loved. She'd been an unbearably lonely young bride sitting out an interminable war with their baby as the only company. She'd been a house-bound mother, waiting for the terrible cable, wondering if, not when, he would come home. Every letter might have been the last. Would she have told him she felt unloved, abandoned by the man who enlisted just weeks after their wedding? Did she tell him the name of Jean's father? There is nothing on the public record. Some years later, when Permella was asked about baby Jean in a public forum (we'll come to that) she replied simply that she 'had got into trouble' while her husband was away. She wasn't pressed for details, and didn't elaborate.

It's not hard to imagine Bill's shock, anger, and disillusionment. His last period of leave to visit London early in October 1918 was granted after he'd received Permella's letter. How could he maintain the self-discipline needed to engage in deadly hand-to-hand fighting? I think Permella expected her husband to judge her badly. She knew the rules. Women who stepped out with men while their husbands were at war were not only disgraceful slatterns, but traitors. She should have been waiting at home for however long it took, chaste and faithful, an exemplar of gracious forbearance. Permella thought Bill would want to be rid of her as soon as possible.

According to the one piece of available evidence—from Permella herself in an affidavit in 1926—Bill said none of those things. According to her, he wrote saying that he would forgive her and that 'things would be alright'. In the years that followed, she would come to see she was a fool to believe him.

Bill was impatient to get home, but he had to wait his turn. With an acute shortage of ships, it wasn't easy to get nearly 200 000 men home to Australia. The sick and the wounded had priority, followed by those who had been away longest. It took the best part of a year—and 200 voyages in 137 different ships—to get almost everyone home.

Word came through that his young brother, Syd, had left Blighty for Australia on 20 November 1918 (*Courier* 26/10/1918). Gassed in April 1918, and then shot in the leg, Syd had been sent to the Suffolk Military Hospital at Hampton and convalesced at Sutton Veny. Bill would have been annoyed, not because he resented his brother's good fortune, but because he had hoped to catch up and ask him to make inquiries about Permella, if possible even to find out the father of her child. The 22nd Battalion, meanwhile, stuck in France, played football, attended classes, and otherwise twiddled their thumbs.

Syd came home to a hero's welcome early in the new year (*Courier* 29/1/1919). He would have had a happy reunion with his parents, Bill thought. There was no unfaithful wife and misbegotten child to greet him.

Bill even felt some empathy for Harry Matheson when he heard he too was steaming home. A dark question came into his head: was it just coincidence that Permella and Connie were pregnant together? Could it be, even, the same man? The two women had been living together. For now, though, he had to cool his heels and wait for a ship.

On 17 December, the battalion took a three-day march from Boulogne into Belgium, and planned to camp for two months at Gourdinne. Generous leave was available for men to spend time in Paris, Brussels, and the UK, but Bill was impatient with all that. He was relieved when orders came for 60 men from the 3rd Reinforcements, including Hughie Kelly and him, to move to AIF HQ on 25 January in readiness for transfer to England and then home. The battalion historian might have been a little more tactful when he wrote: '… as each draft marched out copious tears were shed by the mademoiselles of the village' (Gorman 1919: 118).

Having arrived at Weymouth on 30 January, where he was examined by doctors and found to have 'no disability', Bill expected to be on a ship forthwith. They'd been transported to England just in case a ship was available, but there was no ship. An officer told him it could still take months. He was furious. He'd signed up to serve 'until the end of the War, and a further period of four months thereafter…' That four months had expired; yet here he was still in uniform, saluting and obeying orders, performing mindless drills and parades. On 12 March, he was 'crimed' for 'Conduct to the prejudice of Military Discipline in that he did absent himself without a reasonable excuse from a Parade Ordered by his Commanding Officer'. Hughie Kelly faced a similar charge, and twice failed to appear at the defaulters' roll call. Bill and Hughie had nothing to lose. The commanding officer saw their point. He fined them nominal amounts and confined them to barracks for a couple of days.

Finally, on 8 April—six months after the armistice—Bill, Hughie, and the remnants of the 3rd Reinforcements sailed for Melbourne on the *Tras os Montes*. Three years and nine months earlier, he had sailed on the *Anchises* with 150 men of the 22nd Battalion. Only 59 of these men had come through to the bitter end. During the war, 45 were sent home early, badly wounded or otherwise medically unfit. The other 46 had been killed in action or died of war wounds or disease. Among the survivors, hardly a man had not been hit or seriously sick, patched up, and sent back to the trenches.

They'd been away from their loved ones, their neighbours, their jobs for years, but it would be another six weeks before the *Tras os Montes* docked at Melbourne. Some had great expectations and renewed hope of going back to school or training, new jobs, a settler's block perhaps. Some simply wanted to take up where they'd left off all those brutal years ago. Others nursed injuries no medicine would heal.

The men who had sailed on the *Anchises* back in August 1915 could talk about friends killed or missing in action. These men had been out of the front a month before the armistice, but they had stories to swap about soldiers killed right at the end, some shot on the very last day, the very last hour, of the war. Most units had ceased hostilities well before the 11 a.m. ceasefire, but there was a story about a German shell hitting the kitchen of an Artillery unit at 10.38, killing 14 men. The Artillery retaliated, firing their last shot at 10.59. Pity the poor sods, on either side, killed in those final minutes.

Some men chuckled over brief episodes of flirting and picking up 'filles de joie' on the boulevards and cafés. Married men said they tried to resist temptation, but after all, when every day might be their last, they hadn't gone to Paris to go to church. They said boys became men in the trenches, but they became men of the world in Paris and London. They laughed at their lost innocence as they sailed home.

They cried, too. What could they tell those who hadn't been there when they got home at last? Gallipoli, Fromelles, Pozières, Bullecourt, Passchendaele: ordinary places on a map, but to the men who had been there, they would remain bizarre places where they saw—and did—unspeakable things.

People would say returned men had done their bit for the Empire, and had done Australia proud. No doubt about that, but would a man hold up an empty sleeve and say it was worth losing an arm for? Would a man who saw his brother blown up be forever the keeper of his brother's children? Would a man who had lost his faith on the battlefields ever believe in anything again? Would a man who said this was the war to end all wars, and believe it with all his heart, stand up and urge his children to do it all again next time?

And Bill Sinnett, the grandfather I would never meet? Could he believe that peace would bring back what war had taken away? The closer the ship got to Australia, the more unsure he must have become.

Having simultaneous pregnancies in the one small house had created tensions for the sisters-in-law, and Permella's sister, Margaret, asked her to come live with her and her husband, Henry McCarthy, until her baby was born. Women make mistakes, Margaret said. So do men, said Henry, who had just enlisted—better late than never, he was told. Margaret saw Permella through the birth and helped look after the new baby for a time. Pleasant Street it was, on the corner of South Street. Pleasant Place, she called it. Just right for a lovely baby girl, Jean Adams.

After the birth, Permella went again to her parents' home at 18 Ripon St, Ballarat, with Frances and Jean. She hoped their steadiness would quell her nerves as her husband's return approached. On 6 May, her stomach churned when the AIF told her that he was expected in about two weeks' time. The *Courier* (10/5/1919) pinned it down: his ship would arrive at Melbourne on 18 May. While Permella was increasingly apprehensive, I know how excited Frances would have been to learn that her father was coming home. She was now nearly four, a long time to be without a father. How could she have known what a father was? I imagine Frances did her best in all her naivety to tell her six-month-old sister, Jean, about her dada coming home. I wonder if Frances noticed that the closer the troopship brought her parents to their reunion, the more apprehensive her mother became.

15

The war was not over

I picture Permella in May 1919 in the rain on the dock at Port Melbourne and Bill stands among the troops crowding the deck of the *Tras os Montes*. Guts tightening as they come closer to meeting again. Writing her confession had been the hardest thing Permella had ever done. Now, facing her husband was going to be even harder. Confront and be confronted. It must be done on the wharf, alone, not at the formal gathering at the depot in Sturt Street. That was for happy families and friends. How would she find the words? A brief flirtation that went too far? A vulnerable moment? Feeling abandoned? Loneliness? Flattery? Recklessness? Who knows why we do things that end in remorse?

Frances had never met her father, but Permella thought they shouldn't meet during this reunion. There would be tension, anger, possibly even violence. She had left Frances and baby Jean at home with her sister Margaret. Frances would have to wait another day to see her Dada. She would have thrown a tantrum. Permella and Bill had much to say to each other first, as husband and wife, not in front of a child, nor in the crowded depot in the full glare of his pals. There, the welcoming committee had created a ceremony. Speeches had been prepared assuring these heroes that they would be looked after with jobs, houses, blocks for farming, and pensions for those in need. Permella's agenda was more urgent than speeches.

Word came through that the ship was behind schedule a further three hours because of the weather. The men wouldn't disembark until after six o'clock. Gloom began to fall amid the steady rain. Visibility became poorer by the minute. An official appeared out of the falling darkness and told Permella they had arranged for all the men to be conveyed to a meeting point at the depot in a cavalcade of 100 private cars organised by the Royal Automobile Club. Like everyone else, he said, she'd have to make her way to the depot, quickly. She found cars had jammed the entrance to the pier. As the leading car of the convoy came into view, thousands of excited family members rushed forward on to the road. The procession came to a standstill and it took the full force of the military police to restore order. Many relatives had trouble finding their man in the dark. Some of the returning heroes jumped out of stationary cars and made their own way home (*Argus* 23/5/1919: 6).

Now just one of the thousands straining intently for the sight of a loved one, Permella appreciated that the chaotic mass reunion with self-absorbed groups around each soldier provided the privacy she had thought would not be possible. When at last she spotted Bill, she was shocked by his appearance. He had departed nearly four years ago, still not 21, with a spring in his step. Now ashen-faced and gaunt, he moved slowly in her direction. She may have thought he was hesitant and unsure how to greet her, but the truth was, he wasn't fit enough to move any faster. He hugged her tightly. They declined the offer of a lift by a convoy car. Once his leave pass was signed off—a miserly week they allowed—they caught the cable tramcar to the hotel in Spencer Street where Permella had booked a room for the night.

She had tied herself in knots of negative expectation. She had prepared herself, needed to explain, wanted to offer a defence to rebut the imminent assault. Now alone at last, she expected him to rip into her. She was stunned to find him calm and composed. She asked for forgiveness. He placed his finger across her lips. He said he too must beg forgiveness. We're none of us without sin. Something deceitful had happened, but he had seen much worse. Done far worse. Put all that away, for now.

None of us without sin: whatever had he done? Permella must have wondered, from time to time, about his sexual activity while he was away. She'd heard the many stories about men queuing up at the brothels of Egypt, France, and England. Few soldiers ever wrote home about the practice, but it was common knowledge (Gamage 1975: xv). She'd heard the jokes about the horizontal refreshments supplied by joy-girls. Was he willing to let bygones be bygones because his sin (whatever it was) somehow cancelled out hers? She'd expected him to run the standard line of the day: the sexual lapses of women were more disgraceful than those of a man '...because the offence in the woman's case causes more harm ... and more rapid and permanent injury to her own more delicate moral and intellectual fibre' (Spearitt 1988: 26). Billy Hughes was roundly cheered at Ballarat, when, without so much as a nudge or a wink, he gave voice to the common sentiment that men's sins could be forgiven in the circumstances: 'Australia had bred in the Anzacs a race of heroes, though not of saints' (*Argus*, 13/11/1919: 7).

Permella had known that it would be impossible to keep the news from him when her pregnancy could no longer be concealed. Had her letter of confession been the only one? Who else had written to him? His mother—who never approved of their wedding in the first place? His brother, Samuel—the pot calling the kettle black? One of his sisters, or her own? Not Connie, her mentor and accessory, surely?

Bill gave nothing away. It was too late to worry about that now. Judging by his calm self-control, Permella could have been excused for thinking the long slow journey home had given him the time he needed to adapt to the situation. He understood her situation and saw that what she had done was just one stupid moment in nearly four years without him.

It's pointless—and probably tasteless—to speculate any more on the reunion in the hotel. They had been apart for years. But it is clear from later evidence that Permella left the next morning confident everything was going to be all right.

Next day, they caught the train to Ballarat. Permella's sister, Margaret, and the two children were at the station. I wonder how it was for my mother on that first day when she finally met her father. I can imagine him giving her a big hug, tossing her up in the air, squeals of delight as he caught her on the way down. And Jean Adams? I think he would have given her only a momentary glance as they clambered aboard a tram to take them to Margaret's house in Pleasant Street. They would all stay until the military could arrange Bill's discharge. They needed to find a place of their own. I wonder among the excitement if Frances noticed the tension in the household.

The AIF wasn't finished with Bill Sinnett yet—and he wasn't yet finished with the war. After his week's leave, he met the repatriation Medical Panel. They checked his heart, lungs, and chest. They noticed his wounds where shrapnel had been removed. I wonder if he ever showed them to my mother. The doctors said the scars would cause him no problem—and they were probably right. But he told them he had shooting pains in his right groin. They immediately suspected VD. The test showed his urine was clear, and the pathologist found no other symptoms. Quizzed about his injuries at the front, he told them about Pozières—the trench falling in on him and about being pulled out from under the wreckage. No, he had not been sent to hospital. His sergeant simply gave him a smoke and a tot of rum, and sent him back to work. The doctors looked at the terse medical report they had been given—it said only that sandbags had fallen on him—and probably thought he was lying.

The doctors also scanned the medical reports about his wound in Gallipoli, which confused a gunshot wound and a sprained ankle. They could find no lasting effects from his old wounds. However, they noticed his limp and measured his legs. The left was half an inch shorter than the right.

You must have broken it.

No, that's not true.

There's nothing we can do about it, anyway, so get on your way. Tell the next man to come in.

The medical panel recorded that he was incapacitated by 10 per cent and the medical board endorsed that finding. His injury was due to military service, they agreed, but it wouldn't be permanent. There would be improvement 'in nil to six months'; his 'working capacity [was] affected at present one quarter.' It recommended 'discharge as unfit for General Service...No further hospital treatment desirable'.

With that report, Bill Sinnett would not be entitled to a military pension. He seethed—and he was not alone. One Sydney newspaper (*Smith's Weekly* January 1922) dubbed the Repatriation Commission 'the cyanide gang'. Its medical examinations were designed to eliminate men who may have been entitled to pensions or other benefits. If a man's wounds didn't bleed, the doctors said he was in good health (Dennis et al. 1995: 499). Bill must have felt he had done his best for God, King, and Country, but now that trinity gave him the bum's rush. If he had died—been among the 'fallen'—he would have been acclaimed and mourned. Was there no honour for a man who came home damaged?

Bill talked to other returned men at the pub. They had no time for the Repat doctors, just as they had no time for the fat generals whose only battles were with their receding hairlines and widening girths. It was no consolation to Bill to hear that a tree had been planted in his name in the Avenue of Honour. Fat lot of good that was for him or his family. You can't live off a tree, can you? They gave you medals, but medals wouldn't rid you of the nightmares. The shrapnel scars, the shortened leg, the limp would be a more valid memorial than a tree or medals.

Frances would have been too young to notice at first, but in time she would have come to see her father drank a lot. She would have seen the way he shouted at Permella when she asked for help with the children. He helped sometimes with Frances, but he would have nothing to do with Jean. Frances was not allowed to use that word 'sister'. He called Jean 'that bastard'.

Bill Sinnett was clearly not well. He slept fitfully. When he complained of lice, Permella washed the sheets and blankets thoroughly, but he insisted the lice were still there. Sometimes he sat up all night to avoid his nightmares. Other nights he got out of bed and went walking about the town as if in search of something, or someone. He would not speak to Permella—and certainly not to Frances—about why he screamed in the night. I wonder whether he was having flashbacks about the fear in the face of a young German soldier as he thrust the bayonet through his neck. The Sergeant Major at Etaples taught by the textbook. Not into his chest. The point of the bayonet goes into his throat—like a knife through butter.

Four to six inches. If you drive the bayonet home into the ribs, you have to fire a round to break up the obstruction.

Can a wife ever imagine the man she loves thrusting a bayonet into the guts of another man? Could my mother as a child imagine her father doing that? Wives and mother read the lists of men killed at the front; but did it occur to them that husbands and fathers killed men too? That was their job. How could a man do that job for years without coming home with brutal memories? Where could he find shelter from the shrapnel of his war? His cheeks burned red with self-loathing.

In the morning, Permella called in a doctor who found Bill curled up in bed, in no mood to talk. What was the point in talking to someone who hadn't known the relentless noise, the smell of terror, steaming red blood spilling over cold black mud. Like the Repat doctors, this quack couldn't see the four long years of bestiality buried deep in the soul of a soldier. Wounds once bled had healed, but the war was not over. I wonder if Permella told the doctor—or anyone else—that Bill had slapped her, hard, whenever she pleaded with him not to open another bottle of beer.

The doctor pronounced him 'melancholic' and prescribed complete rest and sleeping draughts. Get over it, man. Your troubles are just nerves. Put the past behind you and get on with your life.

Bill Sinnett insisted he wasn't ill: if anyone was ill, it was the bloody lunatics who ran the war. The science of killing men had improved in leaps and bounds during the war, and doctors had learned a lot about how to deal with maimed and mangled bodies. But men came home with unknown demons hitching a ride in their kitbag, and the doctors were blind to them.

As if the butchery and pals lying in foreign graves wasn't enough, Bill nurtured the fury of deceit at home. For the great cause, he had put their love on hold—and was betrayed. He shared a bed again with Permella, but he began to mock and hector her. For better for worse, for richer for poorer, in sickness and in health, to love, cherish, and obey, till death us do part. A farce.

Permella recoiled at his fits of rage and violence. She was frustrated by his refusal to talk about his experiences at the war, and his anger at what happened while he was away was relentless. But she was not yet willing to give up on her man.

16

Discovery may disappoint

I now find it easier to understand why my mother wouldn't talk to me about her parents. It must have been distressing to watch her father torment her mother, undermining her self-respect and dignity. Young Frances must have been hurt by what she saw—and by other cruel incidents she didn't witness but suffered in their aftermath.

My mother would never have known that written records existed about her parents. I discovered these records in official archives, but gaining access to them was quite another matter. Even though the main characters were long dead, a battalion of bureaucrats defended the 'privacy' of the family they had often disparaged. In their bunkered desks fortified by rulebooks, public servants dusted off the documents to judge whether they were fitting for me to read.

Yes, they told me, we have records about the divorce of your grandparents, and yes, we have adoption and wardship records concerning several of their children, but not about your mother. But you cannot have access to these records, they said, because you don't have the written consent of the people concerned. With the patience of a saint, I provided evidence that Permella died in 1972. I couldn't find a death certificate for Bill Sinnett, but I showed them his birth certificate that indicated he would have been (then) approaching 120 years old. My point was taken, but the gatekeepers were not yet satisfied about my right to the documents. What about other next-of-kin, they asked? They created a perfect circular argument. I had to show there were no other grandchildren with a greater right to the records. How could I do that if I couldn't see the records to find the names of any surviving siblings of my mother? How could I gain consent of people who may not even exist?

As a last resort, I made a formal application to the Victorian Supreme Court for access to the file relating to the divorce of my grandparents (Supreme Court at Ballarat 3/1926). I had no idea what such a file would contain, but I assumed it must have had a bearing on the story that Permella and my mother wouldn't talk about. After a delay of some 18 months, Justice Harper handed down a ruling in which made these comments:

> *[I]t seems to me that the descendants of divorced couples should after 81 years (the period that has elapsed in this case) be entitled to know something about the circumstances of that divorce. Of course, the information may not be pleasing to them, save for such satisfaction as may come from having the relevant knowledge where before there was mere speculation. But it is for them to decide whether they wish to take the risk that what they discover may disappoint* (Harper 2007).

As I turned the pages of the file in the court precinct, I quickly understood what Justice Harper meant. The information was certainly not pleasant, but I was able to put aside 'mere speculation' and confront the narrative in those pages. The key document was a lengthy affidavit lodged by my grandmother in 1926 giving a chronological account of her turbulent life with Bill Sinnett. I found the language of the document clinical, detached, and dispassionate. Her lawyer obviously had a large hand in preparing the text, but I have no reason to doubt the substance of what Permella asserted—other documents confirm all the essential claims she made.

Bill Sinnett did not contest the divorce and did not respond to her version of events. I wish he'd given his side of the story, but there's nothing in the file from him. I wonder whether my mother could have added anything to her mother's story—or given a different slant on the events. I can't imagine my mother would have understood much at all when her father first came home from the war—she was only three and a bit. But as time wore on, she would have seen and understood some of the tragedy that led to her parents' acrimonious divorce. Could she have been a reliable eyewitness?

Permella was patient and tolerant beyond belief. Her written account of their life together after the war shows the extraordinary efforts she made to try to make a go of her marriage. According to Permella, the troubles really began as soon as they moved out of her sister Margaret's house in Pleasant Street in 1919 to a house of their own in Urquhart Street in Ballarat. She had expected things to improve, but they didn't. Bill spent some time playing with Frances, but he tired easily and was restless. He sulked and picked at his food, and when she asked for suggestions, he just grunted. He sat on the front veranda reading the *Courier* and yelled at Permella when she asked if he would fix the back door, which was off a hinge. When he did venture out, it was to the Royal Oak in South Street to meet a pal from the *Anchises*. He often came home the worse for wear, and shouted at Frances and Jean. One night, he lashed out and struck Permella a blow to the cheek. It was not the last time he would assault her.

Bill became increasingly hostile and confrontational about Permella's baby. One day when Jean was crying, he screamed, 'Put that damn child down the shitcan'. Alarmed, intimidated, yet guilt-ridden, Permella began to consider what would soon become an inescapable decision. There were plenty of women in those days who gave up babies born out of wedlock. Given no support from government or family, many young women could see no practical alternative. Sometimes 'giving up' a baby was the last thing they wanted. Young single mothers were usually coerced or manipulated into 'relinquishing' their baby who was then put out for adoption, given to a foster mother, or placed in an institution. The process was shrouded in silence, well out of the public gaze (Senate 2012). Most of these other mothers were young and single—not like Permella. Nevertheless, like many young single mothers, Permella came to feel she had no choice. If she wanted to keep her husband, and a father for Frances, she must make this sacrifice.

On 29 July 1919, an officer of the Neglected Children's Department came to the house to collect baby Jean. Permella should think herself lucky, she said, many a young single mother had her baby taken away at birth with scarcely a chance to look at her child, let alone hold it. Permella had had her baby for eight months. She was supposed to be grateful for those crumbs of consolation. I imagine her sitting by the window long after Jean was carried out of sight.

And Frances? What did she make of seeing her baby sister suddenly taken away? What was she told? Did anyone offer her any comfort? Did her mother's family rally around? I think she got no comfort from her father: her mother had brought it on herself. Her infidelity annulled her right to grieve. The battle was between her mother and father, but did anyone think of Frances?

The Welfare completed the formalities to make Jean a ward

of state, and then looked for a family who would foster her—or 'board her out' to use the language of the day. Permella's sister Margaret suggested a married couple, Ellen and James Wall, who were childless, and practically neighbours of hers. Ellen, aged 38, had a modest greengrocery business and James, 54, was a miner. The Welfare approved. The baby who 'would never know a father's love' would become a 'treasured inmate of a happy home' (Swain, 2012).

The very same day that Jean was taken away, Bill got surprising news from the Repat. He would be getting a pension after all, but only as it related to him, Permella and Frances. The Repat records are confusing—amounts written down in red ink, then scratched out, new ones written in, then crossed out, and yet other red figures taking their place. A hierarchy of red hats waiting up the line for a turn to change the decisions of their subordinates? At first, beginning the following week, Bill would be paid 7/6d a week plus 3/9d for his wife and 2/6d for Frances—13/9d all up (that's just over $50 in today's money). Jean is invisible in the pension paperwork. Bill had disowned her in his application. How could a soldier explain a new baby to the Cyanide Gang when he'd been away for years? Perhaps Bill complained that 13/9d wasn't enough to live on, because a few weeks later the total pension was raised to 19/4½d (equivalent to $75). Not enough to live on still for a family with no employed breadwinner.

No amount of pension would compensate Permella for the loss of her baby, but she thought at least her sacrifice would lessen the hurt that her husband felt, and lead to an improvement in their relationship. She was wrong. Within days of Jean's departure, Bill came home drunk, lost control, and knocked Permella to the floor. It was her turn now to feel betrayed. She had done what her husband wanted, but it made no difference. She hurriedly gathered up a few possessions, including Frances, and rushed to her mother's house.

Three weeks later, Bill came knocking at her door. He had thought long and hard about what he'd done, he said, and begged Permella to come back. She was confused. Why go back when he was still drinking? She was terrified by his rage and the risk of being knocked around again. Yet … there was still love. She hadn't told him yet, but she was pregnant again. This baby was due almost nine months after their reunion at the Port Melbourne docks. Surely the new baby would repair the damage and strengthen the bond between them. Perhaps life could be normal again. Permella also had to think of Frances, now nearly four. Before the split, she used to talk with her father and there were many good days when they seemed happy getting to know each other.

Bill Sinnett was finally discharged from the AIF, too, and there were good prospects for him to make a decent living. Margaret talked to her husband Henry McCarthy who had been best man at their wedding back in 1915. He had recently arrived home from Egypt and he and Bill talked about setting up a wood-merchant business together. Henry had embarked too late to get the front, but he had spent time in training camp, so he was fit and able to do the heavy work. Bill could look after the sales and delivery. He could see a future for himself at last. This was a far better prospect than the one his own father offered. Edward Sinnett had long cherished a scheme to involve his three sons in a piggery business. Years earlier, he had asked the Town Council to register his home as a place of noxious trade. When one by one his sons enlisted, Edward withdrew his application. But, in April of 1918, with Samuel home and in civvies, and a glimmer of hope that Bill and Syd might be home before Christmas, Edward resubmitted his application (*Star* 16/4/1918; 5). He was soon to learn that Sam, Billy and Syd were no longer the boys he fondly remembered. There would be no piggery.

Permella decided to give Bill another chance—on the condition that he cut down on his drinking, and look harder for work. He did make an effort. He asked the Repat to help him, although they questioned his reliability. He told the Repat that he had been employed as a horse dealer when he enlisted; but the Repat saw his enlistment papers showed that he was a labourer when he enlisted.

Fearful of further violence, Permella arranged for the family to live in a shared house at Dyte Parade with other family members—his sister Minnie and her husband Bert Allen and three children, and his brother Syd and his fiancée Thelma Morrison who were planning their wedding. Minnie was older and better able to smooth things over with her brother. Bert Allen was someone he could talk with man-to-man because Bert knew what it was like to have a wife who was once unfaithful. There would be safety in numbers and strong family connections to placate Bill. Many years later, we Goldings lived in another house in that same street. They were small cottages. I wonder how the Sinnetts, Allens, and Morrisons all squeezed in. The little cousins shared beds presumably.

Thelma and young brother Syd had set an early date for their wedding, 23 August. The Salvation Army Citadel was a break from the tradition of ceremonies at the Town and City Mission. But another Sinnett tradition was being upheld. Thelma's condition was already obvious—their baby eventually arrived on 21 December, Frances' fourth birthday.

Syd and Thelma asked Minnie and Bill to act as witnesses at the wedding. Permella believed that Bill would see his young brother's wedding as another stage in the fresh start. Oldest brother Sam—still going by the name of Henry—came from Melbourne for the wedding, alone. Where was his wife, Annie May? Otherwise engaged, was all he would say. The wedding went well. Bill had been drinking only moderately—until he and Henry went outside together. When he returned to the reception, Bill's mood had changed. He refused to say what was the matter, and got steadily drunk. Henry was seen hurrying off towards the city. He would not be seen again for ten years.

Back home, Permella struggled to put Bill to bed, again. He would be 25 next week, but he looked like a man twice his age.

The story emerged eventually, and can now be tracked in public records. Sam Sinnett was in a spot of bother. It would be soon over, he said, if the family could give him a bed for a couple of weeks. He needed to lie low while everything blew over. The month before Syd and Thelma's wedding, Sam had been arrested and charged with deserting his wife, Annie May. Now, as if that wasn't trouble enough, he was ordered to appear in the Supreme Court as co-respondent in the divorce of his mistress, a married woman with two children. Sam Sinnett and Beatrice Little had been living together in Sydney after Bob Little, a Ballarat man, left for the war in 1914. He didn't tell Bill that he had posed as Mr Little to sell their house in Ballarat before taking Beatrice and the proceeds (*Age* 11/9/1919: 11). When Bob Little got home, he caught Beatrice and Sam, with their feet not quite on the floor.

Bill's anger was like a hammer to Sam's head. How dare he presume to ask his help in such a cause? Didn't he know what it means to have another man playing loose with your wife while you're away fighting for your country? The bloody nerve. His own brother thinks it's all right to play around—and expect support. There would be no refuge for a rat like him. This was not the first time Bill had felt disenchanted with his older brother. He recalled Sam's attitude when they met in the hospital in Egypt. It struck him then that Sam was doing all he could to avoid going to the front. Yet they made him a corporal to lead from the front, just as he had done when Bill was a little boy. In those days, he was someone to look up to, a perfect big brother. Bill had rabbited on to his pals at Gallipoli and the Somme about how great it would be if his big brother could be in their battalion. Now this brother was gadding about like a dandy, wearing a ridiculous wig and cheating with another man's wife.

Sam bit back. War's a mug's game. We didn't fight for God or King or Country. We fought for the notables on the other side of the world. It was easy to whip up frenzy and hysteria. We got sucked in. And we all rushed over there to get shot at.

Well, why had Sam put his hand up for the Boer War? The South Africans had nothing to do with us either, so why had he put in two years there?

It was time for some straight talking, Sam conceded. He was never at the Boer War. They gave him two stripes when he enlisted in 1915. No one checked his fictional Boer War record at the time.

Bill was astounded. Sam's Boer War was all a lie? If he wasn't in South Africa when Bill was just a little boy, what was he doing all those years when he was away from the family? Their mother, Alice Sinnett, had told everyone that he was fighting in South Africa for more than two years. It was all a pack of lies.

The bare details of the story can be found in the *Victoria Police Gazette* going back to August 1898. The saga began when Ah Lin, a miner of Main Street, Ballarat East, reported that a silver hunting lever watch and a plain gold band ring had been stolen from his hut. The Ballarat East police recovered the stolen goods and issued a warrant for the arrest of 'a lad named Samuel Synnott'. They described him as about 16 years of age, 5 feet high, medium build, fairish complexion, thought to be living in Richmond.

In a separate incident in October, a Percy Sinnett had been arrested for stealing a horse. Percy was Samuel, using an alias adopted to avoid arrest for the theft of the watch and ring. Percy was the name of his baby brother who had died earlier that year with severe diarrhoea. The magistrate regarded Percy's horse rustling as youthful exuberance, and let him off with a caution. But his arrest for stealing that horse was a black mark when he was arrested by the Geelong Police the following month. They told the magistrates that 'the defendant did feloniously steal take and carry away a silver watch and chain and a gold ring in all of the value of 30/- [over $200 today] … and a tent of the value of 9/- [about $70]'. The magistrate showed no leniency despite his age. He sentenced Sam, just 16 years old, to a month in the Ballarat gaol.

When Sam's time was up on 17th December, he expected to be sent home for Christmas. Instead, not only did they keep him in gaol until Christmas Eve, he was then handed over to the Department of Neglected Children—like his father before him. Under the *Juvenile Offenders Act* 1887, any prisoner under the age of 18 was to be sent to a reformatory.

Sam was devastated. He'd committed a crime and, like a man, had done the time in gaol. Now he would be locked up as a boy in the Bayswater Reformatory until he was 18. It wasn't fair. After three days, he leapt over the wall, just as his father had done before him. On 20 February 1899, he was arrested at Ballarat for 'behaving in an insulting manner in a public place'. His record was growing. In court on 16 March 1899, the magistrate sentenced him to another month in prison, the last two days to be in solitary confinement, presumably to take a good hard look at himself.

Samuel Sinnett's day in court was not yet done. After the lunch adjournment, he faced another charge together with three friends, James Allender and the Bowerman brothers, Walter and John. The four boys had pushed open the door of Ah Wah's hut in the Chinese Camp at the rear of the Red Lion Hotel on Main Street, Ballarat. Sam threw mustard over Ah Wah, and his accomplices pelted him with stones. Stoning 'the Celestial quarters'—to use the language of the day—was a notorious game for Ballarat youths. Twenty years earlier, the local paper described how 'a body of some two hundred larrikins' had stormed the Chinese Camp but were beaten off by 'the Celestials' armed with 'pikes and other weapons of Mongolian warfare' (*Star* 2/1/1879: 2). It was just a lark and Sam fancied his chances of getting off with a warning. Moreover, his 13-year-old nephew, Victor Bennetts (the son of Permella's sister, Lizzie) did his best in the witness box. He swore he was with the youths at the time and Sam was innocent. Sam's hopes rose when James Allender and John Bowerman were given only seven days each and Walter Bowerman 14 days—and all sentences were suspended on good behaviour bonds for 12 months. However, the magistrate would not overlook Sam's three prior convictions, including the one that very morning. He would serve another month, including another two days in solitary confinement. The magistrate then called for Victor Bennetts to be brought back. Although he hadn't been charged with any offence, young Victor was put in prison until 7 p.m. for 'gross prevarication' (*Courier* 17/3/1899: 5).

Escorted back to Bayswater, a reformatory run by the hard men of the Salvation Army—the inmates called them the Starvation Army—Sam was instantly recognised as an escapee. The superintendent took his cue from a Christian colleague, the boss of the Boy's Training Farm at Tally Ho in Burwood, the Rev. George Cole.

> *If they try to run away, as a rule they never try it a second time, for a little mixture of the strap with the gospel, flavoured with common sense, soon puts an end to all that nonsense* (qu. in Howe and Swain, 1993: 62).

Rev. Cole's favoured method did not work on Sam. On 11 December 1899, he again jumped the wall in the company of John Hunter, a 17-year-old from America. The police described Sam as '17 years of age, 5 feet 7½ inches, medium build, light-brown hair, has a sore on little finger of left hand; wore working clothes'. Using the alias Edward Stokes, derived from the name once inflicted on his father, Sam celebrated Christmas with John Hunter in the Castlemaine area. Freedom was again short-lived. Desperate for food, Sam stole a pair of spectacles and sold them for sixpence. The buyer had second thoughts. He knew the spectacles were stolen, and took them to the police, whereupon, despite his demonstrated public spirit, the man was charged with receiving stolen goods and sentenced to 24 hours imprisonment. Getting wind of this news, John Hunter, Sam's fellow escapee, headed for Melbourne and, it is believed, went to sea.

This was probably the time when Sam invented a more acceptable life fighting the Boers. His claim to have been fighting in South Africa for two years and four months was chronologically possible only if he had been overseas by January 1900. But on 6 January 1900, Sam was arrested at Castlemaine, and charged with larceny. Sam confessed that he had stolen more than a pair of spectacles and took the police to where he had hidden other stolen goods—two pairs of boots, a pair of shoes, and a drum. Sam was soon on his way—not to the Boer War—but back to the dreaded reformatory (*Mt Alexander Mail* 10/1/1900: 2).

On 12 July 1900, Sam jumped the reformatory wall a third time. Once more, his freedom was short-lived. By 31 July, he was captured at Ballarat and returned to the dreaded Bayswater for yet another flogging.

Having finally served his time in juvenile detention, Samuel Marsh Sinnett was keen to cover old tracks and make a fresh start. He moved to Tasmania where on 17 March 1908, as Henry Marshall Sinnett, said to be born in Bristol, he married Annie May Ryan. He retained that name for most—but not all—of his later life. It was under the name of Henry Sinnett that Sam was being pursued for his part in the divorce of his paramour, Mrs Little.

Bill Sinnett had become increasingly bitter. He downed his sorrows: disillusioned by the big brother he had always looked up to; betrayed by his wife; angry at the Repat; irked by long delays in setting up the wood merchant business; unable to get any other work that he was physically able to do. At the pub, he pooled his many grievances with those of other returned men: the government had reneged on the benefits they promised; jobs they thought would be theirs didn't exist; veterans were begging in the streets. Strikes and lockouts, violent demonstrations, and sectarian divisions lingered after the conscription debates. Other men may have found ways of coming to terms with their rebuffs in post-war Australia, but Bill turned inward and became fixated about failings—his brother's, his wife's, everyone's including his own.

Soldiers were crowding out the divorce courts, and he pored over the stories in the newspapers. 'It is nearly always the same sordid story,' the *Argus* reported.

> *The soldier returns after four years' fighting to be confronted with his wife's infidelity. A whisper from a neighbour, a chance overheard sneer, the discovery of an incriminating letter – and the mischief is done. Often the erring wife has furnished even more tangible evidence and had to confess to the motherhood of a child only a few months old…*
>
> *Many cases are the sad finale to a hasty enterprise lightly undertaken only a day or two before the soldier left Australia. With one eye on the romance of the situation, and the other on her soldier man's separation allowance many a girl rushed blindly into marriage. The war went on. She spent her allotment on new clothes, her time with new loves. And the Divorce Court is the end.*
>
> *There is something peculiarly revolting in the story of the stay at-home who shows his gratitude to the man who is fighting for him, enduring torment for him and risking death for him, by betraying his wife. Yet as the records of the court show, this has happened over and over again* (*Argus* 22/11/1919: 6).

Bill couldn't have put it better. It was his story as the mug.

It was Sam's story as the opportunist co-respondent. The Little vs. Little divorce story exposed all the sordid details—the unscrupulous malingerer, the wayward wife, and the not-altogether-lilywhite husband. Mr Justice Hood had soon heard enough. He closed abruptly, granted a decree nisi, and awarded all costs against Henry Sinnett (*Argus* 11/9/1919: 4). By any name, Samuel had paid a pretty price.

Infidelity at home was one side of the story. The iconic hero, Albert Jacka VC, told the other side of the story. There were many a 'wronged wife'. He spoke publicly about the temptations offered Australian soldiers in the months following the armistice. The *Argus* elaborated (22/11/1919: 6):

> *The fever of war was certainly responsible for a forced and fictitious state of mental and moral excitement. The absence of rational recreation and the tragic uncertainty of the morrow, combined to induce a tendency to regard evil as more than sufficient for the day. In a sense the war itself was so enormous a crime against humanity that the big sins of normal times appeared small in comparison.*

Permella wondered whether her husband was the only injured party. She remembered that Bill had asked her forgiveness. Why? He admitted nothing. She was left to speculate. A soldier in a foreign country could take whatever pleasures came his way, knowing it might be his turn for the final count the next day. The dreadful 'uncertainty of the morrow'. Permella knew about the birds of prey: the Delilahs, lurking up every murky lane in London. She'd heard the stories from France: soldiers fathered children and went home not caring a hoot about the abandoned mother and child.

Whatever his sins, Bill could never really accept that his

wife's wrongs cancelled out what he had done. A wife far away wouldn't have suffered from a man's philandering in a distant land. A wife playing up here in Australia while he was fighting a deadly war in a foreign land deserved to be eternally damned for her treachery.

17

Chances galore

Permella came to realise, too late, that baby Jean was not the only impediment to peace. She had paid too high a price when she gave Bill Sinnett what the local newspaper headlined "Chances Galore" (*Courier* 18/8/1926: 12). At the time she gave up her baby, she believed they could recover from the calamity the child represented.

On 3 March 1920, Permella gave birth to Minnie Marguerite Sinnett, named in appreciation of the respite that Bill's sister Minnie had provided while she was pregnant. The house would light up with joy again. Frances could use the word 'sister' freely now without incurring her father's wrath. She could dress her new sister like a doll and teach her to talk and walk. Seven months had passed since Permella had handed Jean over to the Welfare and the Wall family. This new baby would purge his bitterness. He took time off his new-found work on the railways to register Minnie's birth. Perhaps he'd been celebrating too well, again. He gave the registrar incorrect information for the birth certificate. Not only had he supplied the wrong date for the parents' marriage, he also listed Hilda Frances as Lily Frances. But his failure to include Jean Adams as Minnie's sibling on the certificate would not have been an oversight.

Permella's divorce affidavit shows that this period of happiness was a short-lived illusory peace. One day, home from the pub, Bill declared that Minnie Marguerite was not his child. Why not? Because it was a girl. If Frances, then 5 years old, heard that, what sense would she make of it?

Permella was baffled. Despite the tension over Jean, it's clear that in the days and weeks after their reunion they slept together intimately. Minnie was born almost exactly nine months after Bill arrived back in Australia. Yet, now he was insisting she was some other man's bastard child.

Emotional cruelty and physical violence became more and more common. At first, Bill didn't hit Permella when Frances was with her, but eventually it made no difference. How did the young girl cope with the strain of hearing her father insist that baby Minnie must sleep in her pram in the kitchen, and not in a bedroom? How did she cope when Permella got up to attend to the crying baby, and Bill exploded and slapped her across the face?

When Minnie Marguerite became very ill and was rushed to the hospital, Bill was outraged that he hadn't been consulted. He issued a bizarre order: Permella was not to visit the child in the hospital. I'm pleased that Permella refused to accept such a heartless command. She bundled Frances up and they went to live at her mother's house again. It must have seemed odd to Frances that Permella went out every night. Later, Permella revealed that she visited her husband every night to make sure he was fed. And, to use the language of her affidavit, they 'had congress'.

After a month, Minnie Marguerite was well enough to leave the hospital and, despite Bill's erratic behaviour and violence, Permella decided to give him another chance. He took her and the two girls to a house he had rented in Clayton Street, Ballarat East, not far from his parents. All seemed to be fine for a couple of weeks until on 2 May, a friend and workmate named Cecil Mitchell, the yard foreman at the Ballarat East Railway Station, found the dead body of a newly born female child wrapped in several layers of brown paper in the bushes near the Levy railway crossing, not far from their house. An inquest found the baby died from exposure. The body remained unidentified.

Now it was Permella's turn for nightmares. The abandoned baby must have been Minnie Marguerite. She couldn't see the face of the person who dumped the baby, but she knew who he was. When Bill asked why she screamed out at night, she couldn't bring herself to reveal her fears, and made up a story—something she'd read about the war. That triggered more turmoil. Bill had been trying to forget the war, he said. How was that possible when everyone around him wanted to have nightmares about it? He detested the pomp and circumstance when the Prince of Wales opened the new Arch of Victory on 2 June at the Avenue of Honour where he and thousands of other Ballarat soldiers had a tree in their honour. 'Blast the trees! Blast the flamin' war!' Everywhere he went, the war was in his head.

Connie's divorce from Harry Matheson made matters worse. The newspapers again lamented the easy-going attitude to divorce. Fifty years ago, women looked upon divorce as a crowning disgrace, the *Argus* reported. Nowadays many regarded it as the natural means of escape from bonds that had become unpleasant or irksome. Familiarity seemed to have bred complacence (*Argus* 22/11/1919: 6).

Connie's marriage had long been intolerable. Divorce would be no 'crowning disgrace' to her. She was still only 25, and had plans. In court in Ballarat in June 1920, Harry Matheson's lawyer was instructed to rip her character to shreds. There was to be no concession to the recent deaths of both Connie's ex-nuptial babies, Francis Sinnett in January 1918 and Douglas George Peace Matheson six weeks after Harry returned from the war.

Harry could have saved his time—and his solicitor's fee. Connie didn't bother to defend herself or her former lover. Charles Lees was nowhere to be found. She knew Lees had enlisted in 1914, had deserted in 1915, and wasn't seen in uniform for the rest of the war. He'd left Ballarat, and their love affair was long over. Yes, she had lived with him for a time during her husband's absence. Yes, he was the father of one of her two wartime children. Yes, she had admitted as much to Harry's brother, John. The Court heard that Charles Lees was the tenth of eleven children in the Lees family. They lived at number 58 Victoria Street, Ballarat. His sister, Nellie, lived at number 48 with her husband, John Nelson. Connie and Harry lived across the road at number 53 with Harry's mother. The gossips all knew there was 'funny business' going on with Connie, Lees, and Nelson. Connie's second ex-nuptial child, Francis Charles Sinnett, was known 'by adoption' as Nelson. John Nelson went missing at the end of the war and didn't return to Australia until 1921. His belated explanation was that he was visiting relatives in Ireland. His wife, Nellie, sneered. The gossips salivated.

Connie scowled with contempt when Harry gave Mr Justice Mann a far-fetched account of his own war career. He presented an image of a heroic Anzac, but he wasn't a clever liar. If Justice Mann had read the long letter Harry wrote to the AIF the following month when asked to explain his multiple enlistments and aliases, Harry may have been back in the court for perjury. Connie didn't bother to raise the matter of his repeated desertions, his recurring VD, or his self-inflicted wound in March 1918 that ended his days in the trenches. She didn't contest his story about coming home from Army camp in October 1914 to accuse her of infidelity. She agreed she'd thrown her wedding ring at his face. She didn't mention that he missed the troopship twice. She had no wish to complicate matters by raising issues about Harry's character. She knew he had a steady girlfriend. He had set his course towards Rose Bond long before his outrage at Connie's unfaithfulness. During the war, he had asked Rose's father to take Connie's place as next-of-kin. And he had informed him about his intention to take proceedings in London to divorce Connie.

Connie and Harry shared a simple purpose: to be rid of one spouse to take on another. She was happy to be portrayed as the sinner and to let him portray himself as the aggrieved—as required by the legal hypocrisy of the day (James 1979).

After his sister Connie's divorce, Bill became even more sullen. He'd seen his brother Sam's dirty linen washed in public in the divorce of the Littles. Now here were the salacious revelations of his sister's divorce. He reminded himself that Permella and Connie were cosy friends when both he and Harry Matheson were on the Somme—and heartlessly betrayed.

Did Frances understand any of this tumult now that she was 5 years old? I wonder if her father ever thought of her in the war that he was waging. She was an innocent casualty of the brutal assaults on her mother. Permella probably did her best to shield Frances, but she was overpowered by events she could not control.

One night the week after Connie's divorce, without notice, Bill Sinnett issued a stark command. 'You clear out of this,' he shouted at Permella. 'I've got someone coming in who will do me better than you.' Permella tried to calm him down, but he jostled her out of the house, into the darkness, and slammed the door in her face. Permella somehow found her way to her mother's house again with Frances and Minnie Marguerite.

In spite of Bill's erratic aggression, Permella persisted in trying to find ways to save their marriage, but nothing she said would shift his belief that Minnie, like Jean Adams, was another man's child. Permella agonised for weeks. She knew that Frances would be devastated, but made a gut-wrenching decision, again. She would give up Minnie, just as she had given up Jean. The Neglected Children's Department was happy to take another 'unwanted' child to put into the hands of a 'good' family.

I wonder whether Permella ever explored another option. Rather than handing Minnie Marguerite to strangers, could another member of the family have taken her in, if only on a temporary basis? That would have allowed Permella and Frances to maintain contact with Minnie. Provided time for Bill to come to his senses. Kinship care, although not as widespread as it is today, was a common enough practice at the time (Qartly, Swain & Cuthbert 2013: 2). During the war and in the aftermath, Permella had sought and received help from a range of family members. She'd lived at various times with her parents, Bill's parents, his sisters, Connie and Minnie, and her own sister, Margaret. Connie and Sam were out of the question, each preoccupied with marital problems of their own. And Alice Sinnett was clearly taking Bill's side in the whole affair. But others might have helped out. Did Permella prefer to deal with strangers rather than compromise her dignity within the family? Or did Bill demand that baby Minnie be removed from the family altogether?

On the day of the handover, Bill made his excuses. He was required at the pub. Permella was left to cope alone. She had asked a local solicitor, Mr Lazarus, to handle the matter. There's no evidence that money changed hands—but it is possible. In those days, before adoption was legal, the thriving market in babies often involved a fee (Cossins 2013). Many mothers—with no income and no realistic prospects of work when they had young children—could see no other option. The records show only that, on 13 July 1920, in the presence of an officer from the Welfare, Permella handed over Minnie, not yet four months old, to a couple named Annie May Green and George Joseph Green of 813 Darling Street, Ballarat West. The arrangement was concluded as efficiently as any commercial transaction.

At just five and a half, how did Frances cope? She had had barely time to recover from the loss of Jean when she faced the sudden loss of her second baby sister. How did Permella ease the pain for Frances? Did she promise that Minnie would come back one day? Did she explain how matters were with Bill? Did she ask Frances to help gather up her baby sister's necessities, her clothes, her playthings, and put them in a box ready for the Greens? Did Frances meet the strangers who would be her sister's new parents? Did she have time to say goodbye? Was she there when her father returned from the pub to issue another astonishing command? He insisted that Permella get 'his' pram back. She refused: whatever would he do with a pram? She now knew that her sacrifice of the second baby was going to make no difference. How could Permella love this violent man who had driven her to give up two babies? How could she ever live with him again? And

Frances? I can't begin to understand how my mother coped with this tragedy.

Yet, despite all that anger, trauma, and pain, a few weeks later Bill Sinnett knocked at Permella's door. He had found a house in Talbot Street. Would Permella give him one more chance (his third)? It seems incredible, but she relented again. Although the wounds were raw, it seems they lived together in Talbot Street amiably enough for a time. Here, Bill produced no more outbursts, and they seemed to be getting on well. Frances may have begun to relax in her father's presence.

Permella felt a little apprehensive when Connie, whose divorce had caused Bill so much anguish only a few months earlier, announced that she was to be married again on 20 November. Bill surprised everyone. He was more than happy to act as a witness, along with Margaret. He even smiled when Connie told him that she was only slightly pregnant this time round. He teased her when she announced the wedding would not be the Town and City Mission—the Sinnetts' citadel. She was going up-market to the respectable Barkly Street Methodist Church. He laughed when she told him that her husband, Stanley John McTaggart, was two years younger than her—just like her first boy. A spark of the young Billy was back again.

By now Frances was nearly six, and overjoyed to learn that her mother was expecting another baby. This time, I imagine Permella desperately wanted it to be a boy—as would

Frances. Sisters brought only misery. Jean and Minnie were lovely babies, but they had wrecked the family. Her father was angry with girls. Frances would look after a baby brother and keep him happy. And her dad would be very happy too.

Nine months after handing over Minnie Marguerite to the Neglected Children's Department, Permella gave birth again. Did hearts sink when it was another girl? Alice Joyce (they called her Joyce) was born on 1 April 1921. It was no April Fools' Day joke when Bill announced, 'That's not my child—it's not a boy.' Permella said she tried to be patient and reason with Bill. She reminded him of their life together at the time when Joyce would have been conceived. He would have none of it. He had been away, he said. He'd been sick. He would never trust her—or any woman—again. The argument went nowhere. It never did.

Drained by this futile quarrel, Permella went to bed early, leaving Bill brooding in the kitchen. She was just nodding off when he burst into the bedroom and shouted, 'Get out of that bloody bed. I am not the father of that child.' Startled, Permella got up and tried to get to the door. He moved towards her. She fainted. When she came to the following morning, she was back in bed. Bill was contrite. According to Permella, he said, 'If Mum comes up today, don't tell her anything, and I'll try and behave better in future'.

He did try. Apart from another move in August from their Talbot Street house to one in South Street, it was a period of relative peace and stability. However, war broke out again on 13 December 1921. The declaration was abrupt: 'I've finished with you. Clear out.' And as if to humiliate Permella further, he repeated the announcement he had made before she had relinquished Minnie: 'I've got someone who suits me better coming in to take your place.' Permella packed her things again and hastily dressed Frances and Joyce ready to leave. Bill pointed to Joyce. 'You can take that bastard, she's not mine; but you can't take Frances. She stays with me.'

I wonder how Frances felt to be hauled off by her deranged father. She was ten days short of her sixth birthday, and utterly powerless. I assume her father never considered a child had any right to a say in matters of control.

Christmas 1921 must have been a wretched time for all. At her parents' house, Permella moped around, attending fitfully to baby Joyce. She missed her little helper—Frances had just turned 6. The thought that Bill would never be able to look after a child so young in his state of mind played on her mind. She guessed, rightly, that he had taken Frances to his mother.

Bill's urge for vengeance had not yet been satisfied. On 8 January 1922, he left Frances with grandmother Sinnett, and turned up at Grandma Adams' house, unannounced. He was there to take Joyce as well. 'I've got someone better than you to look after this child,' he announced again. Joyce was hardly nine months old. Permella reminded him that not very long ago he had insisted he was not Joyce's father. Bill didn't let that inconvenient fact get in the way of exerting his male privilege in an era when children were seen as the property of the father, regardless of the man's competence to care for a child. The best interests of the child and child rights were concepts whose time had not yet come.

Intimidated and demoralised by the fatalistic thought of another unwinnable power struggle for the custody of her baby, Permella surrendered again. Readers might well think she was too meek, but let's not be too quick to judge. The odds were heavily weighted against a woman who was offered little or no support and confronted with a legal system that sided with fathers. Her personal defences had been weakened by the earlier battles, all of which she had lost. A couple of decades on, Frances too would come to know what it was to battle for her children in a patriarchal society.

Bill steadfastly refused to answer her questions. Where was baby Joyce? Who was feeding her? Was she sleeping well? Who was this 'someone better' that Bill had got to look after her? Was Frances doing well? Was she at school? I imagine Frances would have been very willing to tell her mother what she needed to know, but she was not able to leave Grandma Sinnett's house. It must have been bewildering for the 7-year-old who had regained a sister but lost her mother. To be with a father she feared.

After months of depression and isolation, Permella caught a train to the seaside resort of Queenscliff. It was the high season, and she readily found a job as a domestic. The pay was poor, but she had a roof over her head and time to let the tumultuous events of the past months roll around in her mind.

Six weeks later, a letter came from Bill pleading with her to come back to Ballarat and live with him again. He'd sold everything from the old house, he told her, but he would arrange some rooms for them as soon as he could. Permella knew she had given her husband many chances—too many, surely? Since his return from the war, they'd separated four times. Each reunion was a greater gamble than the one before. She would be living with a ticking time bomb.

But what about the children? Frances and Joyce needed a mother as much as a father—if not more so? Bill had had time to think about what he had done—and he could change, she thought. Once more, she capitulated and returned to Ballarat. Bill met her at the railway station. He couldn't take her to the rooms he had secured for them just yet. I find this very painful to write, but Permella's affidavit claimed that he wished to 'claim his rights'—and 'had connection' with her. And those rooms he promised? For the next five months, Bill strung her along with various excuses why they couldn't live together yet. Each time they met, he asked her to be patient. Each time they met, they had 'connection'. The promised rooms never eventuated. Nor would he return Frances and Joyce to their mother. I can't imagine how my mother would have felt about this, but it shocks me to realise that my grandfather was using his children, including Frances, my mother, as bait to turn his wife into his sexual plaything.

18

The runaround

Permella finally brought matters to a head in June of 1922. In her version of the story written years later, she asked Bill's mother to arrange a meeting with him because she had something important to tell him. She would explain everything at the meeting, but she wanted his mother to be there too. After perfunctory pleasantries, she came to the point. She was 'in a certain condition'.

Bill turned to his mother and said, 'Don't you believe her; I am not responsible.' Alice Sinnett was conciliatory for once. She asked her son to be reasonable: 'If it's yours, you should keep the child and look after the girl [Permella].' Bill was adamant: he was not responsible for this pregnancy. How could he trust that woman ever again after Jean Adams?

In the midst of this renewed turmoil, Connie—now Connie McTaggart for the past seven months—gave birth to another child. Tact and sensitivity were never Connie's strong suits. Of all the names she could have chosen for her new baby, it had to be Jean. Bill didn't need reminding, again, that Connie and Permella had played around with other men while their husbands were away.

When Alice Sinnett finally calmed him down, the best Bill would offer Permella was: 'I've got no money at present, but if you keep your mouth shut and don't tell people [the baby is] mine, I'll keep you.' For the months of her pregnancy, Bill visited Permella at her mother's house from time to time and gave her small sums of money—and no doubt exercised his conjugal rights while it was still medically safe.

On 10 December 1922, Permella gave birth to her fifth child. It was a boy. Imagine her triumph! She had held the faith; she and Bill could now make a good life together. She had given him a son, and his old self would return. She thought carefully about names for the baby. He would be Edward Francis Salvador Sinnett. 'Edward' would honour grandfather Sinnett; 'Francis' had been Bill's first choice when Frances was due to be born seven years earlier; 'Salvador' would make an affirmation about the father. This boy—to be known as Frank—would be Bill's pride and joy. And Frances would have a brother at last. That would make her father very happy. Girls had brought trouble in her family.

It was a hard birth, and Permella needed extra time to recover. She didn't leave the hospital until they sent her home on Christmas Eve. She was perplexed that, in all that time, Bill didn't visit. He didn't even show up on Christmas Day. He finally appeared at Grandma Adams' home on Boxing Day. Permella probably thought that male pride had eventually got the better of him. But he didn't bother even to look at his new baby. Permella knew the old signs: her husband was spoiling for a fight.

She tried to discuss practical matters. Would he please give her some money to pay her hospital bills and buy necessities for the new baby? 'You can whistle for them,' he replied. 'I've finished with you for good.'

When they had been reunited after the war, Bill Sinnett said he would forgive her, and they would make a life together. With each new baby—Minnie, Joyce, and now Frank—came another chance to establish that new life. Permella now saw, as if for the first time, that children meant nothing to Bill Sinnett. She had never wanted to see it before, but her husband would never recover. They had no future together.

He was out of love with her. He was out of love with life itself.

As soon as business re-opened in the new year, Permella went to see Mr Lazarus, the solicitor who had handled the arrangements when the Greens took Minnie from her. She would sue Bill for her confinement expenses and maintenance.

On Valentine's Day (14 February 1923), the *Victoria Police Gazette* carried this notice (complete with misspelled names):

> *William Francis Sennett is charged by warrant issued at the instance of his wife, Permella Sennett of 18 Ripon Street, Ballarat with deserting his child. Description given: 29 years, about 5 feet 7 inches, stout build, dark complexion and hair, clean shaven, dressed in a navy-blue suit, black felt hat and tan boots* (*VPG* 23/3/1923).

Bill Sinnett was furious. 'If you don't withdraw this summons,' he said, 'I'll clear out and you won't get anything.'

Permella would no longer be intimidated by her husband's bluster and threats. The matter came before the Ballarat Court of Petty Sessions on 1 March. The bench heard both sides, though there is no transcript so we don't know what was said. Bill was ordered to pay £10 (over $700 in today's values) for the confinement expenses, ten shillings a week ($36) for the support of the new child, together with a surety of £50 ($3 500) to comply with the order. Failure to pay would probably lead to gaol Bill was told. He was immovable. That slattern deserved nothing, and he would pay her nothing. That was the last time Permella—or my mother—ever saw him. And in that moment, I lost any chance of ever meeting my grandfather.

Alice Sinnett supported Bill, her grown-up boy, as best she could throughout. On 22 January 1923, during all this turmoil, Alice wrote to the AIF asking for the medals her son was entitled to: the 1914-1915 Star, the British War Medal, and the Victory Medal. She did not give his address, or her own address, for their return. She explained that he was 'up bush'. Instead, she asked that the medals be sent to Margaret, Permella's sister. Was that a ploy or a gesture of goodwill? Did Alice think it would help the marriage to have the medals sent to Permella's sister who would pass them on to Permella? In the end, bureaucratic rules meant that the AIF wouldn't issue the medals without Bill's written authority—and he was lying low.

Bill's medals would not have helped. Bill was determined to pay nothing for maintenance, and Permella was equally determined that he should no longer shirk his obligations to his children. On 26 March 1923, she caused a summons to be issued for his arrest for defaulting. But Bill had covered his tracks very well. Two years on, Constable Harrison of Burwood told her solicitor that police enquiries led him to believe that her husband had gone interstate.

Bill and his mother as accomplice had played cat-and-mouse games with the whereabouts of the children. The school rolls enable me to track the many moves my mother was obliged to make through the various Ballarat schools (Consolidated Index 1923). She had started at the Golden Point State School, but the day after the court ordered Bill to pay hospital and maintenance costs, she was moved from that school. Two weeks later, Frances was enrolled at the Pleasant Street State School, miles away. Two weeks later, Frances was on the move again, from Pleasant Street School to Urquhart Street State School.

The school was told she lived at 511 Skipton Street. This time, the address was valid. Frances was back with her mother. Bill's parents had become exhausted with the conspiracy. His mother Alice (now 65) and his father Edward (now 69) were struggling to cope with caring for Frances (now 8) and Joyce (now 2). They might have been able to manage the baby, but I imagine Frances was angry and confused about being a pass-the-parcel child, and was a handful. I recall one of the few childhood stories my mother told me. She had knocked a basket of fresh picked plums down her grandmother's well and Alice Sinnett took to her with a switch from the plum tree. In retaliation, my mother butchered three of her chooks.

Alice and Edward decided they were too old to be looking after her without the father's help. Besides, they had to get Frances to school every day. They had to send her back to her mother at Skipton Street. That must have been a great relief to Frances—but she was lost without her little sister Joyce.

It must have been a bewildering period for my mother. Three different schools in the month of March, and more changes in April and May. Her last documented attendance was Urquhart Street School for just two weeks, ending on 7 June. No destination was recorded when she left. I think Permella decided to enrol her in a Catholic school. In another of my mother's rare anecdotes of her childhood, she told me the nuns strapped her around the legs when she was naughty. With the turmoil in her life, I imagine my mother was often distracted at school.

During these years Permella had no option but to tough it out doing the best she could to provide stability without much support. In time, she would be eligible to petition for divorce on the grounds of desertion. On 3 May 1926, her solicitor lodged her detailed sworn affidavit in the Supreme Court in Ballarat. On 18 June, the Court ordered a notice be published in the Missing Friends' columns of both the *Age* and the *Argus*:

> *To WILLIAM FRANCIS SALVADOR SINNETT formerly of Ballarat. TAKE NOTICE that your wife Permella Sinnett has instituted proceedings against you for divorce on the grounds of desertion. Unless you enter an appearance in the office of the Deputy Prothonotary at Ballarat on or before the 17th day of July 1926 and file an Answer within twenty one days from that date the case may proceed in your absence. And further take notice that the sealed copy Petition and copy Citation herein may be inspected at the office of the Solicitor for the Petitioner MARK LAZARUS 42 Lydiard Street Ballarat.*

Permella would now confront the future without Bill Sinnett. She was well aware that some women whose marriages were 'successful' regarded divorce as the 'crowning disgrace', but she could ignore their snide remarks. She was more concerned with the economic hardships that challenged a single mother with small children.

19

Sorrows in battalions

Bill Sinnett did not respond to the 'Missing Friends' notice published in the newspapers. Nor did he show up at the divorce court. He did not contest Permella's account of their life together since he returned from the war. Only one side of the story, then, is documented, but I see no reason not to believe her account.

Taking into account all the circumstances of Bill's behaviour—his violence, denying paternity, failing to provide maintenance as ordered by the court, and his prolonged absence from Ballarat—Permella expected to be granted the divorce and gain permanent custody of her three remaining children, Frances and Frank who were in her care, and Joyce who was still living with Bill's mother. She didn't petition for her other children, Minnie or Jean. She had lawfully relinquished them, although she could have argued that she gave them up under duress. Given her financial straits, whether she could support two more children was another question.

The divorce hearing was set down for 17 August 1926. I think of my mother at that time. She was just ten years old. Shielded from the divorce proceedings, maybe, but she could hardly have been shielded from the news of the terrible death of her baby brother Frank.

On 2 August Permella's cousin, Mrs Olive Lacey, asked her to join her in a drive to see Olive's sister in Lismore that evening. They could stay overnight. Perhaps Permella saw the offer as relief from the stress of the impending divorce hearing. Frances could stay home with Grandma Adams so as not to miss more school. Olive planned to take her two-year-old son, Ben, and Permella could take three-year-old Frank. Olive's friend, Percy Thompson, arranged to hire a car and a driver, Harry White. A third man, Harry Dowie, made up the party of seven, all squeezed into the small car. No seat belts obviously in 1926. Permella was in the front seat with Frank and the two Harrys, while Olive and Ben, and Percy Thompson rode in the back seat. Permella had met the two Harrys for the first time on that fateful day. They later said the men planned to come back to Ballarat the same night, while only the women and children would stay overnight.

They could not have chosen a worse night. On the Rokewood to Cressy Road, heavy rain set in, the road was slippery, and visibility became poor. Only one headlight was working. The car failed to take a bend and plunged into Ferrers Creek. The impact flung Frank through the windscreen into the water. Clambering out of the car, Olive held tight to Ben. Permella searched frantically in the darkness for Frank. Dowie and Thompson helped her. White, the driver, left the scene. After an hour of futile searching, they sought help at a nearby farmhouse. The farmer, Robert Reynolds, telephoned the local police.

Permella must have been in deep shock. Constable Cavanagh said as much to the coroner, a local Justice of the Peace. Like me, this man had to decide what happened without the help of a jury, so it's important that I reveal what the coroner was told. Despite her condition, the policeman said Permella 'was quite rational and was able to give a very lucid account of all she knew about the accident'. She told the policeman she held out no hope of a miraculous rescue. She knew her son had drowned (Inquest report 1926/906: 35).

Nevertheless, Constable Cavanagh went back to the creek with Farmer Reynolds and Dowie to resume the search for Frank's body. Relying on the illumination of the farmer's spotlight, the constable was dragging the creek when Harry White appeared out of the darkness. He staggered along the road and walked right past them. The constable bailed him up and saw that White was in no fit state to help.

'He smelt strongly of drink and I was unable to get any intelligible reply to any questions,' the constable reported. 'I got him in the car and took him straight to Frenchman's Inn.'

The hotel manager undressed White and put him to bed in a pair of his own pyjamas. 'I could smell drink on his breath,' he reported.

They gave up the search for Frank, and Farmer Reynolds returned to his farmhouse and his unexpected guests, Permella, Olive and Thompson. They stayed the night. Reynolds, a teetotaller, remarked that his house now smelled of drink.

The doctor who attended Harry White at Frenchman's Inn around 1.00 in the morning gave evidence that White was incoherent and '...definitely smelled of drink, though he was not drunk...' In his opinion White would have sobered up a bit when he was immersed in cold water.

The diligent Constable Cavanagh decided to sleep at the hotel in order to question White at first light. At 7.40 a.m., White told him that he remembered nothing at all about the accident, but he was adamant that they hadn't had any drinks. He signed a statement: 'We made no stops on the road. We did not stop at any hotel at all but came straight through.'

That story was never going to stick. Percy Thompson was first to break. He admitted they'd called into the hotel at Scarsdale. 'I had a shandy. Dowie had a shandy and White a small glass of wine. Then we had another, the same drinks…' Dowie was next to confess: 'Mr White shouted first. I had a small shandy. Mr Thompson had the same. Mr White had a small glass of wine ... Mr Thompson shouted next. We only had two drinks.' When pressed, Dowie conceded: 'I had two drinks when I knocked off work that day. I had four shandies altogether …'

White was told he could be facing criminal charges, whereupon his memory improved. They'd stopped at the Scarsdale hotel, but it was only to ask directions to Lismore. Confronted by the statements of Thompson and Dowie, he finally remembered that they had spent some time drinking at the Scarsdale hotel. He had drunk two glasses of white port, he conceded. 'They had no effect on me at all,' he said. Constable Cavanagh then arrested White on a charge of manslaughter.

Meanwhile, a message came through that a passing local had spotted a child's body some fifty yards downstream from the car. Constable Cavanagh took Permella to Frenchman's Inn to see the corpse—the constable's word. The constable prepared a statement for Permella to sign:

> *On the 3rd Aug inst. I viewed the body at the Frenchman's Inn at Cressy. I identified this as the body of my son Edward Francis Salvadore Sinnett, born at Ballarat on 10th Dec. 1922. The child was well previous to this accident* (Inquest report 1926/906: 35).

The icy and dispassionate words reminded me of the printed receipt signed by the matron and the driver from the Welfare when Bob and I were delivered to the Andrew Kerr Home in Mornington nearly 20 years later. I was about the same age as Frank when my mother lost her two boys through the actions of our drunken father. The paperwork on both occasions was stripped of sentiment—nothing but the facts. Just facts sufficient to serve the immediate purpose.

I wonder what Permella would have written had she been asked for a statement in her own words. When she got home to Frances, what words did she use to tell her that her baby brother wouldn't be coming home—ever again? Just like Jean. Just like Minnie. And who knows about Joyce? What words would ease the shock, relieve the pain?

The day after the crash, the coroner required Permella to attend a short hearing. He asked her only to affirm her terse statement identifying Frank's body. Then, after hearing a post-mortem report from the doctor—who also confirmed what he had said previously about the driver's condition—the coroner adjourned his inquest until the 20th.

On the third day, Permella buried Frank in the full glare of adverse media publicity. If Frances had access to the papers, she and her school-friends could have read the reports not only in the *Courier*, but in all the Melbourne dailies, the *Sun News-Pictorial*, *Age*, *Argus* and *Herald* as well as the Colac *Herald*. The funeral notice was muted.

> *SINNETT – The friends of Mrs. P. Sinnett are respectfully invited to follow the remains of her late dearly beloved SON, Edward Francis, to the place of interment, the Ballarat New Cemetery. The funeral will leave the residence of his grandmother (Mrs. C. Adams) 511 Skipton Street. This Day at 2 o'clock. A W Hager Undertaker & Funeral Director. (Courier* 5/8/1926: 2)

Grandma Adams made the arrangements discreetly. To the family's surprise, she asked the Catholic priest, Father Gleeson, to conduct the service, and Frank was buried in the Roman Catholic section. Apart from Grandma Adams, Permella was supported only by her brother David, her sister

Elizabeth and husband, and a handful of cousins. Harry Dowie and Percy Thompson, the passengers in the fatal car crash, turned up and carried the coffin (*Courier* 6/8/1926: 7). There was no sign of Harry White—and no one from the Sinnett side of the family turned up.

Bill Sinnett may not have known his son had been killed. He didn't attend the inquest (the first day of which was held 10 years to the day of his own near-death at Pozières).

In that miserable August of 1926, Permella struggled with battalions of sorrows. She grieved for her baby boy. The police were still investigating his sudden death. A man she scarcely knew had been charged with manslaughter. She would be required to give more substantial evidence when the inquest resumed on the 20th of the month. In addition, she was scheduled to appear in the Supreme Court on the 17th to pursue her application for divorce.

I can only imagine the state of Permella's mind when she stood before Justice Schutt. In all the circumstances, I'm sure Frances would have been kept well away. Was she allowed to read the local newspaper report (*Courier* 18/8/1926)? In those days, local newspapers covered local divorces in much more detail than they do today. The judge wanted to know about her children. In the composed language of the formal documents, she informed the court that there were four children 'of the marriage', but one of them 'was killed recently as a result of a motor accident'. The judge asked her about her conduct since 'a certain incident which had occurred while her husband was at the war'. She repeated the substance of what she wrote in her affidavit. She confessed that she had 'got into trouble' and had given birth to a child. William Hovey, a relative by marriage, told the court that Permella 'had made a slip, but had since conducted herself properly'. Hovey confirmed that Bill Sinnett 'did not treat her well while he lived with her' (*Age* 19/8/1926: 5).

The judge didn't question Permella on the claim in her affidavit that her husband had told her, 'If you forgive me for all I've done while I was away, I will forgive you'. I regret to say there's no other evidence to clarify what Bill might have meant—and it seems we'll never know.

At the end of the day, Permella was granted her divorce *decree nisi* with 'costs against the respondent'. I can find no evidence that he ever paid Permella's legal costs, and no evidence that he ever paid for her confinement expenses or maintenance costs during Frank's short life. Little more than a week later—the day before his 32nd birthday—the police removed him from the official list of deserters (*VPG* 26/8/1926: 609).

On the second day of the inquest, the coroner focussed on two issues: the consumption of alcohol and the state of the road. Given the rawness of Permella's shock and loss I wish I knew why Permella took the line she did about alcohol. Yes, she said, they had stopped at Cunningham's Hotel in Scarsdale, but only to ask directions. The men went into the hotel while the women stayed in the car with their children. The men did not carry alcohol from the hotel. No one had drunk anything in the car. No, she couldn't smell alcohol on Thompson or Dowie. White was a careful driver. Her testimony flew in the face of the strong and consistent evidence to the contrary from the policeman, the doctor, the farmer, the hotelier, the other passengers and the driver himself. She conceded nothing and would not apportion blame.

Just as surprising, the coroner didn't challenge her to explain the discrepancy in the evidence about alcohol. In his written report the coroner called Frank 'James'—despite having the name in writing from Permella, Constable Cavanagh and Doctor Carr. Haste causes mistakes, no matter whether they are spelling errors or findings against the evidence. However, the coroner's report troubles me for a more important reason. In the end, his report made no reference to alcohol. Nor did he mention negligence. He brought down a verdict of accidental death. The manslaughter charge was dropped.

The newspapers, which had so extensively reported the death two weeks earlier, hardly noticed the decision (*Argus* 23/8/1926: 19). In the coroner's report, and in nearly a dozen witness statements, I can find no mention of Permella's grief.

After that ordeal was over, Permella might have thought the storm was abating, but the cruel month of August had not finished with her yet. The divorce court, having made no decision on custody, left unresolved the question of what was to be done about Joyce, now aged five. On 26 August, Grandma Alice Sinnett took matters into her own hands. With the formal backing of Mr Sprott of the Ballarat Town and City Mission, she placed Joyce into the Ballarat Orphanage. Alice and Sprott did not consult Permella. I think Permella probably had no energy left for a fight that she might have lost anyway given the prevailing view that a child was a father's possession—even a father who has gone missing.

It's hard to understand why Alice Sinnett took this extraordinary step. She hadn't forgotten that her husband, Edward, had been handed to the Welfare when he was a child. She knew he suffered not just from the traumatic separation from his mother but also from the callous treatment he experienced at the hands of his 'carers'. She knew that he carried the emotional burden of that incarceration for the rest of his life.

The most charitable explanation of Alice's action is that she was convinced that after Frank's death Permella was in no fit state to care for Joyce. If that were the case, she would surely have talked it over with her. If Permella wanted to have some respite to recover from the trauma, a temporary placement in the Orphanage could have been arranged—as many placements were in those days. That would also have reassured Frances, too, that she would see her sister again after a break.

A more likely explanation is that Alice Sinnett was intent on punishing her former daughter-in-law. Alice could recite a litany of irresponsible behaviour to show this woman was not a fit person to care for her son's child. The illegitimate birth of Jean Adams while Bill was away. Giving up Minnie to strangers. Gadding about with strange men on the eve of divorcing her son. And now, the last straw, the reckless death of her only grandson.

The Orphanage Admission Book supports the interpretation that Alice acted with malice. The 'reason for admission' to the institution was left blank. That was unusual. There must have been a discussion between her, her official sponsor Mr Sprott and the Orphanage; yet nothing was recorded. Alice registered herself and Edward as Joyce's grandparents and stated that they were the nearest living relatives. Alice recorded William Francis Sinnett as the child's father, but didn't give the Orphanage any contact address for him. Alongside the mother's name, she entered just 'Permella'—with no surname and no address. Was this Alice Sinnett's ultimate act of dispossession? The woman no longer fit to be a mother was no longer fit to bear the Sinnett name?

Was there perhaps, as well, a touch of sectarian bigotry? It was not by chance that Alice sought the backing of Mr Sprott from the Ballarat Town and City Mission. This was the Protestant agency where Bill and Permella had been married eleven years and a war ago. Permella had enrolled Frances at a Catholic school and Frank had been buried by a Catholic priest. The section of the Orphanage admission form that required the religion of the parents was left blank—the lie you tell when you don't want to state the truth. The protocol between the Orphanage and the Catholic authorities was that young Catholic children would be directed to St Joseph's Orphanage in Sebastopol and then, from school age, to Nazareth House in Mill Street. Did Alice and Mr Sprott see Joyce as a child who might be saved from crossing to the dark side?

The Sinnett family was now further entrenched in the institutions of the Welfare. Edward Sinnett and his son, Samuel, had paved the way. Joyce Sinnett was now the third generation of the family, and the first of the family to enter the Ballarat Orphanage. She would certainly not be the last.

20

The price of peace

After Frank's funeral Permella was never again seen inside the Town and City Mission or the Salvation Army Citadel, the old familiar settings for Sinnett weddings. Becoming a Catholic wasn't necessarily a spiritual matter for Permella. She was closing a turbulent chapter of her life. And having done that, she would attend to greater challenges.

In those bleak times, governments didn't think it was their role to support sole mothers, and divorcees found work as hard to get as married women did. Connie had found a good man after her divorce, and Permella would marry again if she could find the right man. After all, she was not yet 30, and men still found her attractive. Was there a man who wouldn't mind her 'troubled' past? Someone who could restore her faith in men and gentle love?

It didn't take long. As soon as the divorce became absolute in November 1926, John Mahomet Marone, a man five years younger than Permella, moved in as a boarder at Grandma Adams' house in Skipton Street with Permella and her children. I presume Frances was invited to the wedding at St Patrick's Cathedral three months later in February 1927. I wonder if she talked about it with her friends at school. They might have thought that weddings conducted in the sacristy were a second-class sort of marriage (Lord 1954). Why the sacristy? It wasn't a mixed marriage: Jack Marone was Catholic like Permella. Her first marriage had been a Protestant service, which her new church didn't recognise anyway. Perhaps, the Cathedral's reservation was moralistic.

Permella had jested that she was slightly pregnant—as she had been when she married Billy Sinnett. The church frowned on 'shotgun' weddings, even when the bride was 30 years old.

The marriage certificate indicated that Permella had one deceased child, Frank, and three living children: Frances, Minnie, and Joyce. The document did not mention Jean Adams. Perhaps Permella felt the need to keep some episodes of a previous life from her new husband or her new church. I don't know how, or whether, she explained to John Marone why Frances was the only child remaining in her care.

Permella, Frances and John Marone lived in Grandma Adams' house in Skipton Street for years. In the beginning, Frances (at the age of 12) was probably as pleased as Permella was to have a man around the house. In time, however, they both felt they were no better off with this man. When I was in the Ballarat Orphanage and was allowed to visit Grandma Permella, old Jack (as we knew him) was hardly ever there. I didn't ask where he was at the time, and Permella never explained. I now understand why. Jack Marone was not the man Permella was looking for to revitalise her life. His deeds were woven into the web of her secrets.

Little is known about Jack Marone before he married Permella. His early life is enigmatic and the facts in his official records cannot be relied on. He enlisted in the AIF in February 1918, declaring he was born on 19 January 1900. The Commanding Officer at his training camp didn't believe he was 18 at the time, and asked the Government Statist for a birth certificate. The search of the archives for the period 1896-1902 produced no record of his birth. When confronted, Jack confessed that he was just 16½, having been born on 19 June 1902. Even today, no birth certificate exists. In defence of his fib, Jack said that his next-of-kin and guardian, John Mahomet, knew he was under age when he gave his written consent. That excuse cut no ice, and Jack's military service was over in less than a fortnight. If they'd known what was to come in the Second World War, the AIF might have thought itself lucky not to have him in the First War.

In the young man's military dossier, he claimed his parents (unnamed) had died when he was a small child, and he had lived with John and Alice Agnes Mahomet from the age of three. On his attestation form, he described John Mahomet as his 'foster father'. By contrast, Mr Mahomet referred to Jack as his 'adopted son'. The terms 'foster parents' and 'adopted parents' were often conflated in everyday conversation. While adoption was common enough in practice, it was not legally recognised in Victoria until 1928. Alice Mahomet died in 1921 and John Mahomet in 1924, so when Jack married Permella in 1926, he was literally an orphan.

I wonder how Frances felt when Permella was blessed with two babies in quick succession: John James Marone in September 1927 and Catherine Alice Marone in February 1929. Did she feel about young John and Catherine the same way as she did about Jean, Minnie, Joyce and Frank? Or had the constant pain of losing siblings made her emotionally guarded? Maybe Frances, by now an early teen, was too old to sit around playing with babies. Her mother and stepfather certainly needed the income Frances could bring in from her job—at the Lucas woollen mill—but her wages were hardly enough for the family to live on. The adult female wage was set at 54 per cent of the male basic wage, and girls were paid much less than boys.

However, one advantage of being a junior at the mill was that Frances was kept on when many others were laid off as the so-called Great Depression hit. Hundreds of thousands of Australians like Jack Marone were out of work. Susso payments were miserly, and the rates depended on the number of make-work projects that could be funded, and the number of jobless men in the queues (*Argus* 28/5/1930: 7). Life during the Great Depression was desperate for many families. Some lived without hope.

Once Jack Marone saw the futility of queuing for a job in Ballarat, he rolled his swag and hit the road to see if he could make a living elsewhere. He was competing with the large army carrying their poverty across the country. By 1933 about half of all unemployed men had been without a job for over two years (Fraser 2001). There is no way of knowing exactly what Jack Marone did to survive, but there are countless stories of men sleeping rough under bridges, in farm sheds and sports pavilions and spending wintery days in libraries, churches and even public toilets (Cannon 1996).

Permella and Frances made ends meet without a male breadwinner around the house. Handouts and food vouchers from the Ladies Benevolent Society helped a little, but charity came at a high emotional cost. Some of the Benevolent Ladies made no attempt to conceal their disapproval of poor people like Permella and Frances.

War had wrecked many a marriage. Poverty did the same. Permella had watched her first husband go off to war and saw him come back a different man. She now watched her second husband leave to try to earn a living. Would he too come back a changed man?

PART 5
LOST AND STRAYED

I speak of this journey as leading to my grandmother's house even though our grandfather lived there too. In our young minds houses belonged to women, were their special domain, not as property, but as places where all that truly mattered in life took place—the warmth and comfort of shelter, the feeding of our bodies, the nurturing of our souls. There we learned dignity; integrity of being; and there we learned to have faith.

—Elena Georgiou, 2005

21

Abandoned

Frances must have thought she would never see her father or stepfather again in Ballarat. Bill Sinnett had fled in 1923 when the warrant was issued for his arrest. He refused to make any provision for his family—not even for Frances, the one child he unreservedly accepted as his own. The police had given up the search.

Yet, someone had known how to contact Bill Sinnett. I wonder, if it was even Frances. Had he made contact with her after all? More likely it was his mother, Alice, his staunchest ally throughout, who tipped him off about the death of his father. Edward Sinnett had died of stomach cancer on 14 April 1929, aged 75. And Bill, now 35, came back to Ballarat to attend the funeral.

Alice Sinnett was there, of course. So were Bill's brothers, Sam (on his own) and Syd (with his wife, Thelma), and two of his three sisters, Minnie (with her husband, Les Allen) and Connie (with her new husband, Stan McTaggart). Children swarmed around: nieces, nephews, cousins, members of the burgeoning Sinnett and Stokes clans, his father's half-siblings, and their children. The local paper listed more than 30 mourners by name (*Courier* 19/4/1929). But no one from Permella's side of the family, not even Permella.

Much had happened since Bill deserted. His other sister, Lilly, had died of pneumonia in August 1927, aged only 47. Her husband, Stephen Coombes, had found it impossible as a widower to raise their six surviving children. Stephen relied on the oldest child, Alma, who was then aged 16, to look after

William, 13, Nellie, 10, Sydney, 8, Alfred, 5, and Victor, 3. But Alma was a working girl, and it was all too much for her to carry the load. By February 1928, Stephen decided he had no other option than to put his five youngest children into the Ballarat Orphanage.

It is not likely Stephen knew that his niece, Joyce Sinnett, now 7, had been an inmate of the Orphanage for the past eighteen months. Stephen had never known her. He had lost connection with Permella and Alice during the War and in the years of turmoil afterwards. The Coombes children, then, didn't know their cousin Joyce Sinnett when they joined her and the other 200 children in the Orphanage.

A year later, in February 1929, a ten-year-old girl, named Marie or May Green (both Christian names were used in the files) was placed in the Ballarat Orphanage. We now know that the new girl was none other than Minnie Marguerite Sinnett, Joyce's older sister. When Minnie was handed over to the Greens as an infant, Joyce was not even born. They had never met; had never lived together with Permella. They knew nothing of each other. Like Joyce, Minnie was not aware the Coombes children were her cousins. Such was the disintegration of the family, that in the throng of 200 children of the Orphanage, seven of them—Joyce Sinnett, Marie Green and the Coombes children—played, ate, worked, went to the school, and slept in the large dormitories in the Orphanage together. None of them knowing they were biological family.

Why was Minnie placed in the Orphanage? Her mother or father knew nothing about it. Bill Sinnett was still on the run when the *Adoption of Children Act* 1928 formalised what had been common practice in Victoria. Under the law, parental rights were legally dissolved, and whatever communication had been allowed between mother and child had to cease henceforth. Permella had come to believe that she had no legal rights after relinquishing Minnie and Jean although Minnie's foster parents, George and Annie Green, had not yet taken the opportunity under the new Act to formalise the *de facto* adoption that took place in 1920.

The Greens seem to have fallen on hard times during the 'Great Depression'. They told the Orphanage they couldn't continue to look after Minnie because they were in 'bad health'. I think it was not as simple as that. George Green's address was recorded as Bendigo, whereas Annie's was many miles away in Beeac. Were the Greens themselves in crisis? Had they too been victims of the Great Depression? Did they consider asking if Permella was now able to look after Minnie? Perhaps they thought Permella had her hands full with young John Marone, now just two, and with a second child, Catherine, well on the way.

I speculate again about my mother and grandmother at this time. Had they known Joyce and Minnie were in the Orphanage, they could have paid them visits and even arranged for the family to be reunited at last. Taking a longer lens, had my mother learned of her sisters' bizarre situation, would she have resisted even harder when, a generation later, her own three children were being taken from her to live in this same Orphanage? I wonder when my mother first knew we were not the first of her family to become inmates of that institution.

It's distressing to contemplate Minnie and Joyce and the Coombes children rubbing shoulders day by day without knowing their kinship relationship. Had they known, they would have looked out for each other, comforting and protecting one another in that cruel, emotional wasteland of the Orphanage—as my older brothers did for me a generation later. We scoff now at the Welfare propaganda: that children were 'wonderfully cared for by a fine body of men and women'; that the Orphanage was '...in many respects equivalent to up-to-date boarding schools'; that it was 'the finest composite children's institution ... in the world' (*Annual Report* 1935: 4; *Argus* 19/6/1929: 18). In years to come, a formal inquiry heard direct testimony of widespread 'emotional, physical and sexual abuse, and often criminal physical and sexual assault... neglect, humiliation and deprivation of food, education and healthcare' (Senate 2004: xv).

In some cases, a widow or widower remarried, or families did recover from whatever crisis had temporarily disrupted their lives. Some of these parents were able to reclaim a child from the crowded warehouse. The Coombes children were optimistic when they heard that the year after they were admitted to the Orphanage, Stephen Coombes had re-married. However, only one of the Coombes children, Sydney, would eventually return to live with his father and his new wife, Jessie May Hardie, in February 1933. But young Sydney had precious little time with his father who died in January the following year. The system fragmented what remained of family. The other Coombes children were sent out to work in succession when they turned 14 to make their own way in the world. Victor, the youngest, was the exception. He'd been admitted to the Orphanage later than his siblings, and because of some misdemeanour in the Orphanage, the Welfare transferred him, in October 1938, to the dreaded Bayswater Reformatory. At that point, I lost track of him because his Welfare records are closed to the public.

Meanwhile, Minnie Sinnett/Green was released from the Orphanage. In mid-December 1932, after her four forsaken years, a Father Conlan contacted the Orphanage on behalf of her foster mother, Mrs Green. She wanted Minnie back. It took until February 1933 for the Superintendent to agree. By then Minnie was nearly 13. Back with the foster parents who had cast her adrift, she proved difficult to manage. Did she nurse suspicions—as did other children who were abandoned to barrack-style institutional life, and starved of love or affection—that she'd been rescued only because she'd be able to go to work and help pay the rent? Angry and confused by a toxic cocktail of shame, self-blame, and resentment, Minnie was determined not to stay with the Greens.

Unknown to Minnie, Joyce Sinnett, abandoned in the same Orphanage since that painful August of 1926, suffered the worst possible outcome. Even though she was what was called a 'voluntary' admission—never a state ward through an order of a court—her admission card said she would be in 'care' until her 18th birthday. Had Permella known her daughter was an inmate, she could have taken her home. I'm sure that Joyce would have wanted that. When I was at the Ballarat Orphanage, I remember sitting on the high brick wall facing Stawell Street hoping, yearning, to see my mother or father step off the tram that terminated at the Orphanage corner. The wall survives today—along with the memories it arouses.

Sadly, her 12th birthday was Joyce's last. The Orphanage Superintendent told the Committee on 1 August 1933 that she was 'very ill' in the Ballarat Base Hospital. Joyce died in the hospital on 24 August 1933. The death certificate said the cause of death was osteomyelitis, a bone infection. The medical crisis was probably caused by a serious injury that was neglected by the Orphanage staff. There was no inquest. The Committee minute book states that the Superintendent had informed the Committee of the death, 'with deep regret', and 'the President & Members of the Committee attended the funeral.' (Committee Minutes 12/9/1933). The Minutes failed to mention the family. Neither the Superintendent nor the Committee had the decency to notify Permella. There was no death notice in the newspapers. The undertaker, George Ludbrook, the father of the Superintendent, acted as informant for Joyce's death certificate. It names Bill Sinnett as her father but names her grandmother as her mother. He could have got it right if he cared. The details are on the Orphanage admission record. In one final act of neglect, the system expunged Permella from her daughter's final record.

Joyce was the 25th of 26 children who, to that point, died while in the 'care' of the Ballarat Orphanage and were buried over the years in the mass grave set aside for children from the Orphanage. None of the children's names appeared on the drab grey headstone. It simply said: 'Ballarat District Orphanage 1865'. Neglected children, indeed. In 2008, I attended a ceremony arranged by Ballarat Child and Family Services to rectify matters on behalf of these 26 unnamed children. The old weather-worn headstone was replaced by a bright new plaque listing the names, ages, and dates of deaths of each child.

22

You don't know me, but ...

Connie Sinnett had been a free spirit at a time when it was not common for working-class women to show they had minds of their own—especially in Ballarat, a provincial town in more ways than one at the time. As a young woman, Connie was full of fun, carefree and boisterous. I think if I'd had the chance to meet her, I'd have enjoyed her company.

The frenetic years of the war and its aftermath, however, had taken a heavy toll. She had no friends from her days as Connie Matheson, and now as Connie McTaggart she'd been shunned by many of her old Sinnett friends. Even the close ties with Permella had loosened as events pushed them in different directions.

Ready for a fresh start, Connie moved to Brunswick in Melbourne. It proved a tragic decision. In 1932, her husband, Stan McTaggart—like Jack Marone and many other men in the Great Depression—went up bush looking for work. Her son, Thomas Matheson, aged 19, had been unemployed for nearly two years. One day in August that year, Connie herself was out looking for work, and her Jean, then aged 10, was at school. Thomas was the only one at home. The day before, he had received another rejection letter from a potential employer. The coroner may have been compassionate when he ruled: 'a bullet wound accidentally self-inflicted' by the military service rifle Thomas kept in his bedroom (Inquest #1280 8/9/1932).

Connie was never the same vibrant woman again. A long period of withdrawal and isolation was accompanied by a slow and painful illness. She died of cervical cancer in August 1937, aged 41. The death notice in the *Courier* reported only that Connie was mother of Jean and Thomas ('recently deceased'). There was no mention of her other children, all deceased: Mavis Sinnett, Francis Sinnett (known as Nelson), or Douglas George Peace Matheson. I wish Connie had had a better death.

Two months after Thomas McTaggart's death, another of Permella's nephews was killed. This time it was one of the Coombes boys, William, who had been placed in the Ballarat Orphanage after the death of their mother, Lilly. On 29 October 1932, William was driving a car which collided with an express train near Bungaree. His three young passengers were killed instantly, but William lingered on for 12 days. Everyone was distressed by this tragedy, but the newspaper reports made it worse—as they sometimes do. The *Courier* (17/10/1932: 4) reported that the driver of the car was William's father, Stephen. The paper repeated the mistake two days later. It wasn't until it published a funeral notice that the paper confirmed that William had been the driver of the car (*Courier* 31/10/1932: 4).

Although Permella wasn't welcome at the funeral of either of her nephews, their deaths disturbed her. William's death, especially, reminded her of her son Frank's death and caused her again to feel anxious about the lives of her other lost children. She wondered if she would ever see any of them again. She didn't talk about them, but that didn't mean she didn't think of them often. Mothers often grieve for many years over the loss of the children they 'relinquish'—a weasel word covering up coercion or manipulation of a powerless mother (Senate 2012). Permella understood the torment of mothers who were told their sons were missing in action during the war. On 21st December every year, on Frances' birthday, she baked a special cake and they went out to Lake Wendouree or the Ballarat Zoo. But on the 9th of November every year, how could she not think too of Jean? Or Minnie every 3rd of March? Or Joyce every 1st April? Would she pull the curtains and say the sun stung her eyes? Frank was different. Maybe she'd come to terms with Frank's death because she was there when it happened. But the missing girls were different. Wherever they were, how could she look at a girl playing happily in the street and not wonder whether her girls were happy and healthy? Or whether they were still alive?

It is possible that her sister, Margaret McCarthy, kept her informed about Jean for some time after Permella handed her over to the Welfare. I found a baptism record at St Peter's Anglican Church in Sturt Street, Ballarat. The register has consecutive entries for 16th January 1921. The first child is Mary Catherine McCarthy—Margaret's daughter—and the second is Jean Adams. On Jean's certificate her parents are listed as: 'Mother: foster mother; Father: State Child' (Ancestral Detective Agency 1998 #3852, #3853).

Over time, Margaret's contact with Jean declined and whatever little information had been filtered down to Permella ceased altogether. Although Ellen and James Wall didn't formally adopt Jean until May 1933, they had exercised exclusive parenting rights as her *de facto* parents from the first year of Jean's life, and Permella had no parental rights. The Welfare believed that:

> *Every care…must be exercised to keep [adopted children] happy in their ignorance as the disillusionment would assuredly…make the rest of their lives unhappy to learn they, in most cases, came into the World nameless and were deserted by those responsible for their existence (Annual Report* 1935: 8).

My mother's sister Jean Adams, would be forever Jean Wall and kept 'happy in her ignorance'. Permella would have expected it to be a matter of time before her Minnie would become forever Minnie Green. Yet wherever she was, she would have felt that Joyce could come back to her one day. In the meantime, she busied herself with her new children, John and Catherine Marone, both now close to school age. She had no help from their father Jack Marone, who, unemployable in Ballarat, was on the road in search of ways of making a living, less by fair means than foul.

Frances knew she had been the only child her father accepted as his, but that was no great consolation. She had waited years for the war to end to meet her father. He'd been wonderful to her, and then horrible. Before she knew it, he was gone again. Her mother had replaced him with a part-time stepfather, and in place of her three sisters and her brother were a new half-sister and a half-brother. Frances had to cope as best she could with the web of perplexity, grief, and instability.

She turned 18 in December 1933, and, a month later, was a married woman. She needed her mother's consent, which was hard to refuse since she was reminded that she was the same age back in 1915 when her parents had given their consent to marry Billy Sinnett. At least Frances wasn't 'in the family way' and would get married as 'an honest woman'.

Permella met her intended son-in-law Stanley William Robinson only days before the ceremony in the Marriage Registry Office at Ballarat. Reluctant to discuss how he and Frances would have enough money to live on, he assured her that wasn't Permella's concern. Her job was to help with the paperwork. When Permella signed the consent form she added the annotation: 'surviving parent of the bride'. Was that wording conscious irony, or did she know something about Bill's fate? She listed the long dead grandfather, Edward Sinnett, as the father of the bride presumably to avoid embarrassing questions about Bill Sinnett. After the formalities Permella went straight home.

Just after the wedding, a new girl started work at the Sunnyside Woollen Mill where Frances worked until she was put off because the Mill preferred single girls. Workmates told Frances they were struck by the girl's strong resemblance to her. Frances made some enquiries. The new girl's name was Marie Green—some called her May. Frances knew that a Mr and Mrs Green had adopted Minnie, and by her calculation, at 14, this girl was the right age. Frances waited at the gate at knock-off time to catch a glimpse of her. After a couple of days, she tapped Minnie on the shoulder. 'You don't know me, but I'm your sister. If you want to find out who your real mother is, here is the address.' (Personal Communication LR, May 2014).

When Permella answered the knock at the door, she hardly recognised the teenager she had last cradled as a babe in arms in 1920. She would have rushed to hug and kiss her effusively. I imagine Minnie stood awkwardly in her mother's embrace, not knowing what to make of the two small children clinging to her dress.

There was much to talk about, but it would have been hard to find the words to explain fourteen years of separation. Making a new life together would not be easy. John and Catherine Marone watched on, round-eyed with bewilderment. Who was this teenager? Their sister? But where had she been? Questions begat other questions. Jean and Joyce? Frank's death? The father of all these children? Too many questions. Answers would have to wait.

Permella bustled about the house after the miracle had brought one of her lost children back. But Minnie was never truly 'back'. Permella soon began to see that she had her hands full with an angry adolescent, wanting answers. Why had her mother given her away to the Greens, people who didn't love her? Why hadn't those people returned her to her own mother when they tired of her? Why did they abandon her to that brutal orphanage? Why did they take her back again, only to dump her again? Who was her father? Where was he? Who were these other children? When the eyes of a child sting with aggressive resentment, a mother sometimes has no answers.

Permella felt that Minnie's anger would have calmed down if they created a stable life together long enough—without being distracted by Jack Marone and Stanley Robinson. Hard times brought out the worst in Minnie's newly acquired stepfather, and her sister's new husband. Minnie knew all about Robinson, she said. They'd met in the Ballarat Orphanage, of all places. Their time in 'care' had overlapped by only a matter of weeks—he'd been an older inmate from 1927 to 1929—but she'd been none too impressed. Minnie heard that he served time in a reformatory after the Orphanage. She couldn't see what her sister saw in him. As for Jack Marone, Minnie could only conclude that her mother had been desperate to marry. They were both no-hopers, those men, if you asked her. No one asked her, but Minnie would tell her what she thought anyway. Orphanage kids were like that.

Permella was at a loss to know how to respond to Minnie's hostility. Her husband was no help. Jack Marone's drunkenness only made matters worse. When he got his hands on any cash, by fair means or foul, he spent it on liquor. Minnie called him Jack Moron and Jack-of-no-trade. When he threatened to take his belt to her, Minnie skipped out of the house, returning only after she thought he was asleep, or too drunk to notice.

Jack Marone's first conviction—as distinct from his first offence—had occurred in January 1937. He appeared in the Ballarat Court of Petty Sessions on six counts of making false statements. He was given the option of fines amounting to £11/2/6 (more than $900 today) or 17 days in the Ballarat Gaol. He had no money, and so began his intimate acquaintance with what he came to call his Bluestone Cottage. Over the years, he became a regular boarder (*VPG* 4/2/1937: 112). Permella and the Marone children had to cope without him for frequent stretches of time. Minnie said they were better off without him.

Permella's sole income was through the sustenance system (later known as the dole). Minnie's wages (15/2d per week, just over $60 today) at the Sunnyside Woollen Mill helped put food on the table; but what Permella needed was more than financial support. Stressed and tired, she went to bed as soon as the evening meal was over and the dishes were washed and dried. She suspected Minnie was taking advantage of her early-to-bed routine. She was right. Minnie frequently slipped out to meet a boy from work and returned in the wee small hours through her bedroom window.

When her mother finally caught her with one leg through the window, they had the sort of fight that could only be had between an insecure mother and a defiant 16-year-old daughter. Imagine the 'discussion'!

No, Minnie would not change her ways.

Yes she would, or else.

No, she would not stay home every weeknight.

Yes she would, or else.

No, she would not pay Permella more board.

No, she would not stop buying make-up. She'd spend her own money any way she liked.

She'd do as she was told, or else.

Or else what?

At her wits' end, with no one to turn to for advice, Permella went to the city watchhouse. The police might help by giving Minnie a stern talking to. Make her see the error of her ways. I wonder if Permella remembered that when Edward Sinnett's parents asked the police for help in 1865, their intervention resulted in five years' detention for the 11-year-old boy. Minnie's grandfather had been the victim of a system that allowed parents to commit their children as 'neglected'. Decades on, not much had changed. The Head of the Department in Victoria, complaining that the courts were sending increasing numbers of girls to his department, condemned both parents and girls alike.

> *In most of these cases, a lamentable lack of any parental control goes hand in hand with an equally lamentable lack of consideration by the children for their parents' feelings and the good name of the family (Annual Report* 1928: 5).

Permella simply wanted to give Minnie a scare, but she misjudged the close alliance between the police and the Welfare. Once they recognised the Sinnett/Marone family as past 'clients', the system took the matter out of her hands. The Children's Court in Ballarat heard the case of 'Police v Minnie M Sinnett' on 25 January 1937. Minnie stood charged with being a neglected child, as her grandfather had been in 1865—and as Frances' own children would be, decades later.

Edward Sinnett had been just 11 years old, but Minnie was almost 17, barely below the age ceiling for committing a juvenile offence. What was her offence? The prosecuting officer laid out the case against her. There is something particularly gendered in the way facts and moral judgments were assembled. Her mother had 'no control over her'. She wasn't attending Sunday school. The girl had a record of being neglected. She had been an inmate of the Ballarat Orphanage for four years—as if her status was an additional offence. Her mother was 'on Sustenance'—another status the police found offensive. By contrast, the police told the court that her stepfather was 'of sober habits'. Tongue-in-cheek, surely? Jack Marone was finding it hard to get a drink in gaol.

All of the above was troubling, not doubt, but hardly criminal behaviour. The magistrate was more interested to learn that Minnie was 'said to be pregnant probably six weeks.' There was mention of VD, although no medical evidence was presented or asked for. That was enough for the magistrate. He concluded that Minnie had 'led an immoral life' and declared her 'a neglected child lapsing into immorality'.

Teenage pregnancy was common enough in those days. The Sinnett family provided evidence of that. Had Minnie come from a 'better' family, discreet arrangements might have been made to send her away for a decent time to avoid the shame and blame. Minnie had no one to speak for her. The magistrate condemned her for her wickedness, and committed her as a ward of state, despite her age.

The police conveyed Minnie Sennett (that's how they spelled her name) to the Royal Park Receiving Home for Girls in Melbourne. She was then incarcerated at the Oakleigh Convent, or Girls' Reformatory (now the site of the car park at the giant Chadstone shopping complex). There she encountered the gothic discipline that made the Ballarat Orphanage seem like a benevolent asylum. The Nuns of the Good Shepherd made sure Minnie engaged in no late-night frolics. They locked all the girls in their dormitories from early evening until 6 o'clock in the morning when the day began with prayers, lumpy porridge and lukewarm milk tea. Despite her pregnancy, Minnie was ordered down on her knees again to clean the floors and to purify her soul. The Archdiocese weekly spared no praise: '...so polished are the floors...that it would be convenient to take meals thereon' (*The Advocate* 7/11/1908: 18-19). If scrubbing the floors were not sufficient to purify her soul, she was sent out to do a full day's work: washing and ironing in the commercial laundry, rounding up the cows, milking, separating the cream, washing the vats, mucking out the cattle pens, tending to the vast vegetable garden. Given her pregnancy, surely the Good Shepherd Nuns, the 'ministering angels', would have spared Minnie from having her head shaved or being flogged with heavy wet towels (*Age* 27/4/2003: 5).

On 4th June 1937, Minnie was sent to St Joseph's Maternity Home in Grattan Street, Carlton. When Permella inquired about what would become of Minnie's baby, she was told it was no longer her concern. The Nuns would take care of everything, as they always did with 'fallen women'. They had a list of married couples who would take a child born out of wedlock to raise as their own. This 'relinquishment' would shield the family from the shame of it all, and deny the neighbours the opportunity to pry around curtains. Coerced into silence, the young mother would grieve alone at the loss of her daughter who was a made a ward of the state, and then fostered out.

Minnie not only lost her baby to a stranger, she also lost contact with her family outside. The nuns would not allow family visits, even Permella was turned away. News from the outside world, even family news, was carefully filtered. While she was locked up, she did not know that her step-father was in and out of prison. She did not hear the news of Connie's death in August 1937. There was nothing from Frances about her baby Bill who was nearly two years old by now. She did not know that Frances had separated from Stanley Robinson. Nor that she had a new partner, Al Golding, and had another child (Bob, in December 1936). She was not be told when her sister was pregnant again. I was born in April 1938 and I would never meet my Auntie Minnie or the little baby taken by the Nuns, although years later, almost by chance, I would meet one of her other children born later in happier circumstances.

When war broke out in September 1939, Minnie had no way of knowing who among her family had enlisted. As we'll see, nevertheless, the war would touch her deeply.

23

War rages again

It took Frances no time at all to realise she had made a big mistake in marrying Stanley Robinson. Permella wasn't surprised. She didn't pass judgment because it had taken her daughter less time to 'wake up to herself' than she had taken to realize her mistake with Jack Marone. Mother and daughter were in the same mess. Both their husbands had now become what the police call 'persons of interest'.

The evidence is clear: neither Jack Marone nor Stanley Robinson was skilled at their chosen trade, petty crime. In their first year of his marriage to Frances, Stanley went to prison several times—although for minor offences. As the years went by, though, Frances saw her husband's dossier grow thicker. A *Police Gazette* posted his retrospective résumé in 1948: 'Began his career in 1933 as a petty thief, but has developed into a troublesome breaker, who will doubtless continue to offend.' And he did. Over the years, he accumulated convictions for breaking into houses, shops, garages, and factories; receiving stolen property; larceny; unlawful assault; being idle and disorderly; obstructing and threatening police; false pretences; breaching a bond. The list goes on.

Frances had no stomach for that sort of life. She took the earliest opportunity to leave Stanley. Just 19 years of age, she was on her own when she gave birth to her first child, my brother Bill, in March 1935. She still wore her wedding ring which reduced the risk of sharing the misfortune of many other young women without male partners. Her baby wasn't taken from her to be given to one of the respectable mothers waiting in the queue to adopt an 'unwanted' child.

Soon afterwards Frances met the man who would become my father and Bob's. Unfortunately, as we shall see, our mother hadn't seen the last of Stanley Robinson—to her detriment and ours.

Bill Sinnett's brothers, Sam and Syd, had not had enough of war the first time around. They joined up together again in Melbourne in May 1940. They bumped into Jack Marone when he, too, was enlisting. If they chatted a while comparing their experience of the 1st World War, it wouldn't have been a long conversation. Recall that only Syd could speak from direct experience. Sam's war was limited to a free trip to Egypt and return. Jack's military career amounted to a fortnight in camp after being found to be under age.

Sam—or Henry, as he called himself—didn't let inconvenient facts inhibit his wish to enlist. He sliced ten years off his age and told the Army he was a single man living at Eureka Street, Ballarat, with his mother—his authorised next-of-kin, probably without her consent. Henry had gained rapid promotion in the 1st World War based on false claims about serving in the Boer War. Now he gained even speedier promotion on the basis of his dubious service in the 1st World War. Within a week, he was promoted to corporal. Within a fortnight he became a sergeant. And by the time he was discharged in November 1941, being 'required for employment in a reserved occupation'—managing a real estate office—he had risen to the rank of warrant officer. Once out of uniform, Henry

Sinnett didn't go to his mother in Ballarat—that was never his real address. He had other plans.

Permella found this second war radically different from the first. The first had thrown her family into disarray, not only for the damage it did to Bill Sinnett in the trenches, but also for what it did to his family at home, and in the aftermath. In 1915, Permella did everything she could to stop her husband enlisting, but now in 1940, she was better off without Jack Marone. His frequent arrests for drunkenness and petty crime disrupted family life, the more problematic were the fines and lost employment that drained the family's already meagre finances. She needed steady money to hold together what remained of her family—little Jackie and Catherine and her own ailing and frail mother, Catherine Adams. The steady allotment from his military pay would be a blessing to Permella. However, she soon discovered she couldn't rely on her husband's military allotment.

Less than a month after he enlisted, Jack Marone began malingering. His record is startling: overall, he was absent without leave (AWL) on more than 20 occasions, sometimes for months at a time. When he was arrested by the military police, they often found he had sold off his military equipment. Several times, Jack was caught by military police in Ballarat. I wonder if he knew, after all, about the infidelity of Connie and Permella during the 1st World War. Was he checking up on Permella, just as Harry Matheson, the quadruplicate soldier, had checked up on Connie?

Listed to embark for overseas service early in 1941, Marone went AWL again. He was again arrested, but instead of locking him up this time, the AIF put him on to the next troopship bound for the Middle East, in April 1941. For the next year, he so distracted the military police with regular absconding and misdemeanours that the AIF sent him home. Marone jumped ship at Durban, was re-captured, put on the next ship under escort, and eventually transferred to the Sydney docks as a stevedore, loading military supplies. There, in one of his longest stints of continuous service, he worked for nearly a month before he disappeared again. Belatedly, in August 1944, the AIF decided he was 'unsuitable for any further military service'. Before they discharged him, they made him complete a sentence in military gaol on a charge of misconduct. In all, Marone was in the Army for over four calendar years—and was AWL or in military prison on a total of 354 days.

The loss of her husband's pay and fines wrecked Permella's hope of a steady income. She had difficulty paying the bills, and had to move house a number of times, one step ahead of the debt collectors. For a while, she and her two teenage children moved in with her mother at King Street, Ballarat. She'd been the one person who had stuck by her when Frank was killed. Half mad with the stress and humiliation of the inquest and the divorce, Permella wouldn't have survived without her mother managing the funeral and seeing Frank off with some dignity. However, in September 1940, it was Permella's turn to manage a funeral. She buried her mother in the Catholic section of the Ballarat New Cemetery—as we now know, in the same plot as Frank.

Permella was now alone with her two children from the Marone marriage, John now 13 and Catherine 11. With Stanley Robinson long gone, she decided to team up with Frances and her partner, Al Golding. In addition to Bill (now aged 5), they already had two new children, Bob (4) and me (2). If Permella thought she would now have a stable life by connecting to her daughter, she was wrong.

It's a difficult story to tell. In the years we lived together in later life, I could never get straight answers from my mother and father or any eye witnesses. I have had to rely on written documents—which I know cannot be trusted. Sometimes the Welfare records are nothing more than anecdotes that come to be accepted as factual over time because no one challenged them. My father's recorded version of the on-again-off-again partnership with my mother cannot be taken at face value. In their early years together, even before my father enlisted in the Army, they were not consistently together in Ballarat. I have found his trail in Melbourne and Geelong and in his home town of Mount Gambier. His frequent absences from my mother is a multi-layered story. Some of the facts are available, even if their interpretation is disputable.

According to a statement our father made to the Welfare in 1940, he came home from working in Melbourne to find Frances in the company of Bill's father, Stanley Robinson. She allegedly told our father to 'clear out & take the kids' (File No. 66852 3/10/1940). This must have been the extraordinary night of the manic train ride to Melbourne when our father handed Bob and me over to the Welfare. Is it true that our mother told him to take us with him—or a cock-and-bull story? The Welfare certainly made no effort to check our mother's side of the story.

In the files, I found a letter written by my father in April 1941 asking the Welfare to release Bob and me from the Andrew Kerr Home in Mornington and to hand us back to our mother. The Welfare agreed, and placed us on 'probation' for three months. It was proposed that, if there were no problems, we would be formally 'discharged' to her in September.

I've learned since that words like 'probation' and 'discharge' were common in children's files. The language betrays the functional relationship between child welfare and the police which was established in the earliest colonial days in Victoria under the *Neglected and Criminal Children Act* 1864. The structural association continued, in Victoria at least, until 1984 when the child protection function was finally separated administratively from adult corrective services (Jaggs 1986: 176), and the language is more sympathetic. Can we be confident that the ideological remnants of that relationship are nowhere to be found in child protection services?

Not long after we came home to them, our father enlisted in the AIF in July 1941. A few weeks later, so did our mother's husband, Stanley Robinson. Both of her men named her as their next-of-kin. Both made an allotment to her from their pay. It is impossible to know whether she was party to this deception or the unwitting beneficiary of two men simultaneously wanting to show that she belonged to them. I look again at that sole surviving photograph of us as a family. I see the photo in a different light now. Is it a statement of our father's rightful possession of our mother and his boys, including our Bill?

Intentional deceit or not, my mother's double dipping was too good to last. Neither of her men was cut out for military service. Like Jack Marone, they were chronic troublemakers, although they couldn't match Jack when you count the number of times they skipped camp. Both Privates Robinson and Golding were AWL on only four occasions. However, when Stanley Robinson went AWL, he made it count. If you tot up the number of days, his absences were four times greater than the extravagant tally of Jack. Robinson was AWL in blocks of 514, 446, 198, and 98 days. The Army might have discounted 70 days from the first block of 514 days. He was actually on duty for those 70 days, but served under an alias. During his first period of unlawful absence, he took a job on a dairy farm in Minto, New South Wales, far away from Ballarat. When he was arrested for thefts from the farm, the civil authorities were not aware that he was a soldier missing in action.

After he was released from gaol, Robinson thought the best way to cover his absence from the Army was to enlist as a new man. That ploy had worked for Harry Matheson decades earlier in the First World War. From April 1942, Stanley Robinson was known as Private Stanley Warren until he was caught in September 1943. Ironically, he was again AWL at the time of his arrest. The Army charged Robinson not only with his own unlawful absences, but also those of the bogus Private Warren.

During his last period of AWL, the 98 days, the civil police arrested him on a charge of shop breaking and larceny. When he was discharged finally from Pentridge Prison in March 1945, he was finally sacked by the AIF. At war's end, my mother's husband (whether known as Robinson or Warren) had been on military duty for a total of just 162 days spread over three years and nine months of service.

When I put their military records side by side, I noticed that the two men in my mother's life were AWL simultaneously on two occasions in October 1941. On one of these occasions, our father dropped in on Frances and found her in the company of her husband. Their hostile confrontation probably explains our father's alcoholic-fuelled rage as he bundled Bob and me, for the second time, on to the train to Melbourne.

My father represented the situation to the Welfare by asserting that she was with an 'undesirable man who is well known to the Ballarat police'. The Welfare officer took him at his word, not bothering to investigate his story. When he said he didn't wish her to see 'his' children, the officer simply noted his wishes on the file. There was no comment on the implications for us or our mother.

Did my mother know what my father was doing? I can't find any record of her being told what he had done or how she reacted to the sudden loss of her two young children. She knew what it meant to have loved ones taken away without warning. As a child, she had seen her siblings one after the other—Jean, Minnie, Joyce and then young Frank—snatched away. And then her father disappeared. Had she become immune to loss? Did the loss of her own children simply add a new layer of scars to the old wounds?

That second frantic train ride, that second drunken jealous rage, was the start of a very long journey through the Welfare for Bob and me. With the one short respite mentioned earlier, it lasted more than twelve years. Bill, now re-named Bill Golding, joined us for ten of those lost childhood years in the Ballarat Orphanage. I wish I had known then how the pieces of the jigsaw puzzle slid into place. It took me many years to uncover how close was the association, intentional or not, between the Sinnett family and that Orphanage.

My life as an 'orphan' could have ended much sooner than it did when my father was discharged, prematurely, from the AIF in April 1943. However, his discharge was dishonourable—not because of his bouts of absenteeism, but because of repeated drunken fighting with his superiors and the civil police. In late 1942, he had been arrested in a brawl in the streets of Geraldton, Western Australia. He was sentenced to five months in prison by the local magistrate who wouldn't tolerate soldiers fighting in his town. Rather than send my father to fight the Japanese, the Army decided they would have more peace without him.

The Army's loss, unhappily, was not our gain. Wherever my mother was, I was surviving bare-knuckle brawls in the Orphanage where an angry battalion of abandoned boys routinely set upon one another. Under the blind eyes of the staff—and sometimes with their approval—older boys turned on new boys in order to wring some power out of their own powerlessness. The veteran boys bullied the small ones, created entertainment by cajoling the new kids into fighting amongst themselves. Bob and I were sometimes set up for this sport.

In the early years of the 2nd World War, the Orphanage battles were fought on the gravel playing fields and the evacuation trenches that were dug in the backyards of the Orphanage. Those precautionary measures were abandoned when the trenches become waterlogged in the Ballarat winters and harbouring rats (Superintendent's report 13/8/1943). We could again peer out the windows at night to see the enemy approaching: "All black out blinds have been taken off the windows as they were beginning to look very shabby." (Superintendent's report 27/10/1943). The orphanage excelled at keeping up appearances—and at keeping children from 'unworthy' and 'undeserving' parents. We did it tough all those years—but I know now that my mother did it even tougher.

24

Passings

In the final weeks of the war, in July 1945, Grandma Sinnett died in her 85th year. Permella was ready to make peace with the Sinnetts, and wanted to go to the funeral, but two things stood in her way. The disappearance of Joyce was still painful. She didn't want to stir up old yearnings. She hadn't seen Joyce since Frank's death and her divorce. When she had tried to find out where Joyce was, Alice had simply said, 'Don't ask me; talk to Bill.' How would she talk to Bill? She hadn't seen him since 1923, three years before their divorce. She heard he was at his father's funeral in 1929, and fully expected him to come to his mother's funeral. She didn't know how she would react to being in Bill's presence again. Would his anger have mellowed? Could they talk now about things they hadn't discussed when it might have made a difference? In the end, Permella didn't have the mettle to face the combined force of the Sinnett family.

She needn't have worried. In contrast to Edward's funeral, which was attended by all his children, only two turned up to Alice's funeral—Minnie Allen and Syd Sinnett. Her death certificate listed four living children and their alleged ages: Samuel (52, but really 63), Minnie Allen (54), Bill (50), and Sydney (47, but really 45). My guess is that Syd supplied this information, and he was covering for Samuel and their falsehoods when they were enlisting for the 2nd World War.

Permella had always liked Syd. He was different from the other Sinnetts. Unlike Bill, he had settled down after serving in the 1st War, happy in his marriage to Margaret Morrison. They had three more children and led an altogether unexceptional life, by Sinnett standards. The family needed a white sheep.

Permella also had a soft spot for Bill's older sister, Minnie. Her married life with Herbert Allen got off to a shaky start and was never truly happy. She'd been a 'fallen woman'—like her namesake Minnie Marguerite Sinnett, twenty years on. In the year before Herbert made her 'an honest woman' in February 1911, Minnie named her first baby Percival James Crago Sinnett. Mr Crago had been embarrassed—and so was the child, in later life. As a married man with four children of his own, Percy Crago Sinnett decided in 1942 to discard the unwelcome tags and became Percival James Allen. In later years, the volatility of the relationship between Minnie and Herbert appeared to have been transmitted to some of their children. A number of their grandchildren were placed in children's Homes—including that home away from home for the Sinnetts, the Ballarat Orphanage. But that's another story.

I wonder why Bill and Sam Sinnett didn't attend their mother's funeral. Readers will recall only a few years earlier, Sam had told the AIF he was living with his mother in Ballarat, and he named her as next-of-kin. Sam may have been ashamed of showing his face in Ballarat. His shady dealings had continued after his release from the AIF in October 1941. At that time, he claimed to be required for employment in 'a reserved occupation'. His appeared as Henry Sinnett in the Geelong Fair Rents Court in 1943. As manager of a dodgy real estate business, he overcharged tenants and kept falsified records of income (*Argus* 27/1/1943: 3).

Sam's capacity to invent and re-invent himself was so effective that his first wife, Annie May Ryan, only ever knew him as Henry, while his second wife, Gladys Myrtle Billows, only ever knew him as Samuel. When he died in 1952, Sam's death certificate stated that he had been married twice, but the informant could supply no details of his first marriage or his children by that marriage. When his son from his first marriage, George Henry Sinnett, died in 1969, his father was correctly named as Samuel Marsh Sinnett. I wonder whether Samuel learned his skills of manipulation as a teenager incarcerated in various detention centres. As early as 1870, a Victorian Royal Commission had warned that the system of locking up children was hurtful to their morals and led 'in after-life into permanent pauperism and crime' (Victoria 1870: vii). Sam's father had sunk into poverty but not crime, whereas Samuel was never poor.

But where was Bill Sinnett? Was he still alive when his mother died? Syd thought so, but he could have been guessing. Old Edward had been the glue that held the Sinnett brothers together. Once he passed away, the children hadn't much in common and went their separate ways. Alice hadn't heard from Bill or Samuel for many years. Nevertheless, she made a will, leaving the surviving children equal shares of her estate, which amounted to a State Savings Bank account with a balance of £157.5.9d, about $10 000 in today's terms (Probate #365772 31.7.1945). The probate document provides no answer about his whereabouts. Bill Sinnett never claimed his entitlement.

Did Bill know, or care, that his mother had died? Had he effectively dropped out of society? Had he learned from big brother Samuel that a new identity was a practical answer to life's challenges? We'll never know—unless there is some astute reader out there who holds the missing piece of the jigsaw.

If Bill had attended his mother's funeral in 1945, I wonder what he would have made of the men in the lives of his former wife and Frances, the only daughter he accepted as his. Had he learned about their military service, he would have been unimpressed, I think, by all of them. The man Permella chose to replace him? After his volatile career with the AIF, Jack Marone still could not hold down a job and, unlike my father, he continued his long struggle with alcohol, and most of his stretches in prison were related to alcohol and vagrancy. In the 1950s, men were still being locked up for being unemployed and homeless. The euphemism at the time was 'insufficient means of support'—the same charge I faced as a four-year-old in the children's court in 1943. The police and the warders at Ballarat came to know Jack Marone well. Despite his 21 prior convictions, he was an inoffensive prisoner. In the end, he was listed as having 'no fixed address' but it might as well have been 'HM Prison Ballarat'. His son John was his only visitor. It's little wonder that when we (Bob, Bill, and I) were granted day release from our own prison at the Orphanage to visit Grandma Marone, we seldom saw Jack Marone. After the Orphanage, I remember he once came to our house in Main Road Ballarat, drunk and dishevelled. Our father issued instructions: we were not to talk with him; he'd only be wanting money or cigarettes. As teenagers we saw a man in need of a helping hand, he was family, but we turned our backs on him.

Halfway through a six-month sentence in the Ballarat Gaol for vagrancy in December 1954, Jack Marone suffered a cerebral haemorrhage (Inquest 1955/38). He was buried as a pauper in the St Vincent de Paul mass grave in the Ballarat New Cemetery. He had no belongings, no property, nothing to hand down to his children. The coroner assumed that the family was notified. I had just finished Year 11 at Ballarat High School at the time, but my mother didn't tell me he had died. I wonder whether she knew, or cared.

I think Bill Sinnett would also have judged Stanley Robinson harshly, not only for the fiasco that was his military career, but also for his ineptitude as a man of crime. Stanley continued his life of petty crime until 1948, when the courts had had enough of him and sentenced him to two periods of 18 months gaol concurrent, and another 12 months cumulative (*VPG* 20/5/1948). His police trail went cold in the 1950s. Did my mother ever see him again? I don't know. A man answering Stanley Robinson's description died inconspicuously in Melbourne in 1956.

Bill Sinnett might have thought Al Golding the best of a poor bunch, despite my father's alcohol-fuelled skirmishes with the law in his early days. Towards the end of our stretch in the Ballarat Orphanage, he stopped drinking altogether, and he and my mother were able to develop a stable relationship that lasted for the rest of their lives. I've always wondered, however, why my mother never followed her mother's lead in divorcing her first husband to enable her to marry again. They lived for decades as if married. Our mother only ever used the surname Golding. Bob's birth certificate states that our parents were married in 1934, but that was untrue. As late as 1948, when my parents were trying to get us out of the Ballarat Orphanage, the Welfare cited their 'irregular' family situation as one of the reasons we boys could not be returned to them (Golding 2005: 217).

What more could Permella have done to support my mother through her exhausting battles—with Stanley Robinson, Al Golding, the Army, the prison system, and the Welfare that took her children and would not give them back? Permella was a mute spectator of the mayhem that entrapped us in the Welfare from 1940. She'd been a witness when we were rescued from the Andrew Kerr Home in 1941 and when we were locked up in the Ballarat Orphanage in early 1943. Grandma Sinnett watched as we grew and changed as the years rolled by. And she fed us roast dinners at Skipton Street when we had day release. I can now see why she chose to have us remain 'happy in our ignorance' about the reasons for our incarceration. Decades were to pass before it was possible to reconstruct her part of the story.

I can't recall the point in time when we boys from the Orphanage stopped visiting our grandmother at Skipton Street, or when she ceased to play any part in your life, and why. If we'd stayed connected with her in later life, I wonder what she would have told me about her life, her husbands, and all her children. And about my mother.

My mother was caravanning in Queensland in 1972 when her mother suffered a terrible death. She never talked about it. I read the cold, clinical account in the hush of the Public Records Office in North Melbourne (Inquest 1972/1539). The language is cold, businesslike, dispassionate—like the language I found in Frank Sinnett's inquest report. The resident doctor at the hospital saw 'the patient following her cessation of respiration'. The police sergeant simply read from his notes. I suppose that's how officials are trained to do their job. Permella's son, John Marone, at least, showed some feeling in his evidence. And from his words—rather than from my mother—I learned how my grandmother died.

Grandma Permella Sinnett had grown up when electric

light was new in Ballarat. As a child, I remember the lighting of the gas lamps at dusk in her Skipton Street house. Their sputtering was the signal that it was time for us to go back to the Orphanage. When electricity replaced gas, she never fully trusted it, didn't relish the bills that came with it. She removed the light bulbs in her bedroom, preferring to use candles. They were safer, she told her children Jacky and Catherine (who still lived with her as adults). By now a frail 76, she was living in an old weatherboard house at 327 Errard Street, Ballarat. At about 1.30 in the morning of 7 June 1972, she got up to go to the toilet. She usually kept a candle burning near her bedside. On this wintry night, Jacky had put out her candle. Half asleep, she tried to light another. Her tired old fingers fumbled. Her nightie was alight in seconds.

Her screams awakened the household. By the time Jacky reached her, she was rolling about on the floor. Her nightdress was off but her petticoat and singlet were still alight. Jacky ripped the burning clothes from her body, lifted her on to the bed, and wrapped a blanket around her.

They had no telephone. Catherine couldn't leave Mark, her small child. Jacky would have to run to the hospital for help, thankfully only five streets away. He wasn't yet 45, but he was an invalid pensioner, and not fit. Panic drove his legs. He was back at the house before the police and ambulance arrived. The policeman remarked on the strong smell of burnt hair and clothing.

Permella lay in intensive care with burns to her head, neck, trunk, and upper limbs. It would be touch and go, the doctors said. She drifted in and out of consciousness. Jacky and Catherine took it in turns to visit. They could hold the fingers of her left hand, one part of her that was not burnt.

In the fortnight between the fire and her death, Permella

talked apparently—though not always coherently—about her family and life in the old days. Jacky and Catherine didn't understand a lot of what she said. She talked about Frances and Jacky and Catherine. And Jean, Joyce, Minnie, and Frank. And her husbands, Billy Sinnett and John Marone. She was calling the roll, but only Catherine and Jacky answered.

Why didn't her other children come to see her? She hadn't heard from Frances for months. She knew she was away, in Queensland somewhere. No fixed address. The fever rose and fell. At critical points, she was wracked with a hacking cough. She spat up pus. After a while, she lost consciousness and slept fitfully for hours. Some days when she woke up, she didn't know who it was standing around her bedside. Nurses, doctors, Jacky, Catherine—they were all the same, all demanding answers. Everyone was a priest, a confessor, an inquisitor.

On other days, she was open and lucid. She recited a list of the houses she could remember, a catalogue of domestic memorials. The little cottage at Haddon where her parents raised nine children before they moved into Ballarat, where she met Billy. Ascot Street, where she got sick and had to be rushed to hospital. This very same bed, she'd wager. She was number eight on the Adams side, Billy number eight on the Sinnett side. Billy told her the 'Celestials' who camped in Main Road said number 8 was the luckiest number. It brought wealth and happiness. Pieces of eight, Billy hoped. A happy pregnancy brings a happy child, the Chinese greengrocer told her. Dana Street, number 1302. Or was it another house in Ripon Street?

After a while, her parents became just like Billy's—nosey Parkers. Where was she going? Where had she been? Who was she with? Maybe they were right. If she'd listened to them, she wouldn't have got herself into such a pickle.

At Permella's age, burns like that don't heal. Her rasping

cough got worse. Periods of fitful sleep outweighed the periods of confused awareness. When Catherine brought her child Mark to the ward, Permella called him Frank.

I can only presume Permella asked Jacky and Catherine to bury her in a grave with her son Frank and her mother Catherine Adams. Did she also ask that her other children not be mentioned in the newspaper notice? And on the death certificate? Jacky and Catherine supplied family details to the coroner who was the nominated informant for the death certificate. It named her parents correctly including her mother's maiden name. It listed her two marriages and her age at the time of each. Yet, it listed Frances as the only child of the first marriage. Permella was about to be laid to rest with her son Frank, but he was not listed on her death certificate. Nor was Jean Adams (perhaps Jack and Catherine Marone did not know about Jean). But surely, they knew about Minnie and Joyce Sinnett? When I asked about this later, Jack and Catherine refused to comment.

After Permella's death, Jacky and Catherine and her son Mark stayed on in the old weatherboard house next to the Salvation Army Citadel in Errard Street until their deaths: Jacky in 2004, Catherine in 2010 and Mark in 2015. With their deaths, it seems impossible to shed further light on the reasons why the family I found in the Ballarat New Cemetery—and beyond—was so fragmented and disconnected. I regret they would not tell me why their mother had lost touch with all of her Sinnett children, including my mother. I regret that my mother could have told me about the fate of her siblings. They chose to take what they knew to the grave. Would it have confirmed what I have since discovered?

Jean Adams was the only one of the Sinnett children to have a stable childhood. Taken in by the Walls at the age of eight months, she knew no other parents, although she was nearly 15 when they formally adopted her in 1933. She seems to have grown up as the Welfare desired—'happy in her ignorance' of the Sinnett family.

Did my mother attend her wedding in 1940? I doubt it. Even if she knew about it, she had other more pressing matters to deal with at that time. Her children were being put into the custody of the Welfare at the time Jean married Leonard White, a dairy farmer of Cardigan near Ballarat. Their marriage certificate cited Ellen Wall as her mother and James Wall as her father. There was no mention of the mother who gave birth to her, and the identity of her father remained—and remains today—a matter of speculation. In the throes of her meandering monologue on her deathbed, Permella hadn't revealed the name of the man with whom she had 'made a slip'. I'm not sure she would have betrayed him.

If Jean Adams ever learned the story of her first family, what would she have made of the grave at the Ballarat New Cemetery shared by her mother, grandmother and brother Frank? And her sister Joyce in an even more remarkable grave a short distance away? Would she have pondered the fate of her other siblings, Minnie and Frances? What would it have meant for her if Permella had been able to keep her babies?

Permella's relationship with Minnie Marguerite Sinnett

never recovered from its wretched start. Minnie had carried a chip on both shoulders. Resentful of her mother's apparent neglect, she also nurtured grievances about Mr and Mrs Green, the Orphanage, the nuns of the Good Shepherd, and the Welfare. She never knew the father who had forsaken her, just as she would never know her own daughter who was taken from her. I wonder whether her mother ever told Minnie about the part Bill Sinnett played in her decision to relinquish her. Would this knowledge have eased the mother's guilt and remorse and the daughter's anger at betrayal and abandonment?

In time, Minnie might have forgiven her mother for handing her over to the Greens, but would she have forgiven her for handing her over to the police, which was a short step to the children's court—and thence to the nuns, and the loss of her baby? Would it have helped if she'd known that her grandfather's parents had handed him over to the Welfare too? Perhaps not. Minnie was nearly 17 when her mother surrendered her for the second time. Would history have been changed if she'd been given some support from the family, or from the state?

Permella was probably not aware that, once Minnie was in the hands of the nuns in Melbourne, her legal rights as a mother—and Minnie's, too—would be extinguished forever. Minnie would never know the identity of the family who took her baby. Adoption 'closed' the records. The original birth certificate was sealed and a new one issued. The door to the future slammed shut, and was locked.

As soon as her baby girl was taken from her, Minnie was sent to the Sisters of St Joseph at Broadmeadows, where the nuns employed her—without wages—in their commercial laundry. After a while, she was sent back to the Oakleigh

Convent to be trained as a domestic servant with skills in dairy work. The blueprint had not changed since the Girls' Reformatory first opened. The nuns isolated the girls from family and community while they trained them for menial jobs far away, 'it being considered better to send them to situations in the country than to the scenes of their former careers' (*Argus* 4/3/1882: 11).

The 2nd World War created broader opportunities for young women in Australian society, but the common destiny of most female wards of state remained 'situations in the country'. The system had little respect for working class girls who came into the system, especially those who were 'fallen'. The Welfare continued to carry low expectations and to provide limited opportunities for girls transitioning out of their 'care'. On 1 February 1940—just two days before her sentence as a ward was due to expire—the nuns sent Minnie to a Mrs Harrington of Yabba North. The Welfare gave her £5 (about $370 now) to kit herself out and start a new life in the outside world.

No doubt, the nuns had tried to teach Minnie the error of her ways. I'm not sure she was of a mind to learn. Out of sight of nuns and family alike, and amidst the turmoil of another war, Minnie turned 21 and broke free. Calling herself Mary Marguerite Therese Synnett, she met a young man from Shepparton, Hector Norman Beasy and they married in the Registry Office in nearby Mooroopna in August 1941. On her marriage certificate, she claimed her father, William Francis Synnett (sic) was dead. It's hard to tell whether she knew this as a fact or was speaking metaphorically.

The newly-weds had hardly begun their honeymoon, when there came a heavy knock at the door. The bride was shocked to see her groom taken away in handcuffs. The military police had been looking for Private Beasy for some time. Hector hadn't found time to tell his bride he was AWL. The honeymoon was over—and so was the marriage.

Thirty years later, Hector wrote to the AIF with a highly unusual plea for help. He told them he had been serving in Milne Bay, New Guinea, when he was granted compassionate leave in 1943 to instigate divorce proceedings. He thought he'd done so before being re-posted, he said. He had presumed the divorce had gone ahead in 1943. All these years later he found it had not, so he was asking the Army for help to see 'this oversight be rectified'. He had no money for solicitors, and anyway, he wrote, he 'could not consider legal services in this district of my long-standing residence [Mildura], for reasons of privacy' (NAA Series B884, V52344: 21).

Not surprisingly, the Army offered no assistance—this was a civil matter. Norman Beasy had to find his own way to gain a divorce from Minnie, which he finally accomplished in April 1980. Did my mother or her mother know anything about Minnie's calamitous marriage? I was struck by the parallels with the multiple marriages of Permella, not to mention Connie and Harry Matheson, and my own mother's too. Is it unkind to think the Sinnett women had a flair for choosing the wrong men? Or for being chosen by the wrong men?

What became of Minnie's baby? Years ago, I wrote:

> *I have discovered, by means that I am not free to disclose, but the source is reliable, that at five months of age (October 1937), Minnie's unnamed baby girl was committed as a ward of state, charged with the now common family crime of 'being without sufficient means of support'. She was then fostered out to an anonymous family, and was later adopted by them. The files are closed to scrutiny.*

I can say nothing more about Minnie's child. Who knows what name she went by or what sort of life she led? The same mountain of evidence about the impact on forced separation of mother and baby that had applied to Permella as a mother applied equally to Minnie as a mother. Minnie would have been devastated for decades into the future (Senate 2012). And, notwithstanding sweeping claims about adopted children being 'happy in their ignorance', I imagine that as she grew through childhood, Minnie's daughter would have wondered endlessly who her parents were. And the scars that itched would have continued on into adulthood.

In 2013, the Victorian adoption law was changed to allow a mother to have access to identifying information to enable contact if both people are willing. If mother and daughter are both alive, Minnie would be in her 90s, and her daughter in her 70s. Almost certainly, the reform came too late for them.

Then came an unexpected intervention. I had put out feelers on a genealogical website, not with any great confidence of success. After a long silence, a woman contacted me. We checked each other's credentials. I told her Minnie's date of birth and the names of her parents and about her brief marriage to Hector Beasy. The woman then proclaimed we were first cousins. We were both excited. Lorraine had never met anyone from the Sinnett family, let alone a first cousin; and I had found Minnie's daughter, my mother's sister's first-born daughter.

She was not, however, the first-born daughter I'd expected. Lorraine and I met for 'a long chinwag'. She told me she was the oldest of Minnie's five children. Their father was Frank. (Another Frank!) She and the other children knew their mother by name as Mary. She'd been a wonderful mother, and she and Frank were very happy together until his death in 1994. Mary continued to live independently with the loving support of her children until she too became unwell. She died in 2007, just four days before her 87th birthday.

I was not surprised to learn that Mary/Minnie had told her children almost nothing about her harsh early life and about her fragmented Ballarat family. That was the way of the family. Yet, over time, she could not avoid some important disclosures. Some of the older children remember some of Minnie's siblings visiting from Ballarat, and their accounts of these visits gave me new insights.

After the war, Catherine Marone had found her half-sister Minnie living in South Yarra. She'd written to her and had even gone to stay with her for a few days. Later, when Minnie moved to Euroa, Jacky Marone had ridden his motorbike from Ballarat to pay her a visit on more than one occasion. Jacky and Catherine kept news of these contacts from their mother—even on her deathbed—because Permella had forbidden Minnie's name to be spoken in the house. Notwithstanding her own lapse while her husband was overseas, Permella had never been able to pardon Minnie's 'wicked behaviour' as a teenager. In turn, Minnie found it hard to respect the mother who'd betrayed her when she most needed help. Yet, paradoxically, Minnie wanted to be kept up to date with her mother's life. Catherine, it seems, also disliked the way their mother treated her as a child, and was happy to share news and views with Minnie in clandestine letters.

I was even more surprised to learn that my mother, too, had paid Minnie and her family a visit in Euroa. Why had she never told me about that? I was taken aback to learn that she had given Minnie photographs of Bill, Bob and me. Photos we had never seen, photos that Lorraine had now passed on to me. We see the three boys posing outside 140 Eureka Street, Ballarat. This is the last house we lived in—for a time with our mother, and then with Pearl Hills and her five children—before we were taken to the Ballarat Orphanage.

My new-found cousin, Lorraine, was able to pass on family stories she had heard from her mother about our grandmother. She told me that Catherine and Minnie laughed together about their mother's cooking. When she was out of the house, they would pitch her scones at the wall to see how far they bounced. I still thought my grandmother's Sunday lunches were delicious; but I suppose when you're hungry and live in an orphanage the quality of food is not as important as the quantity.

Amusing anecdotes about Minnie were one thing—getting hard information from her was quite another matter, Lorraine told me. 'You certainly were left in no doubt when it was time to stop asking questions.' In that regard, her mother followed the lead of our grandmother—and my mother. Towards the end of her life, however, Mary relaxed the secrecy rule a little after an episode that caused red faces. Lorraine had asked her mother the date of her wedding and, acting in good faith, the children arranged a surprise wedding anniversary party. Soon after the party, Mary and Frank decided to stop living with their deception and finally got married, in 1988. Their five adult children were both surprised and delighted. Towards the end of her life, Mary also felt able to tell Lorraine about her short, hopeless marriage to Beasy and their belated divorce. It was that hapless wedding to the wayward soldier that Minnie's children had inadvertently celebrated!

Lorraine was surprised by what I was able to tell her about Minnie's early life. She had been a loving and caring mother, but she raised her five children very strictly, taking special care to supervise her daughters' social activities. They never suspected that their mother had been a 'wayward' adolescent—'in moral danger' no less.

Another grenade had also lobbed into the family trenches. Two years after Minnie died, Lorraine received a letter enclosing an unknown telephone number and asking her to call. Intrigued, Lorraine called and the conversation went along the following lines.

'Hello.' The voice was strained. 'My name is M and I'd like to talk with you about something personal. I hope you don't mind, but I got your name and address from your mother's death certificate. Our mother's death certificate, actually. I'm your mother's oldest child.'

'No, you can't be,' Lorraine said. 'I'm the oldest child.'

'No, I was born in 1937 and our mother was forced to give me up when I was three weeks old. I've been searching for her for many years. If only I'd known where she lived, I would've been in touch before it was too late.'

Nothing could have prepared Lorraine for what she'd just heard. At the end of the conversation, she sat, stunned, trying to absorb its meaning. After recovering from the shock, Lorraine and her new sister arranged to meet. They had a lot to talk about.

M (I withhold her name by request) told Lorraine that she was inspired to find her mother because she'd learned that Minnie had tried to have her returned to her when she was about four. She had been thwarted by the Welfare who informed her that she had no rights because she had signed adoption papers. 'The gun was pointed at her head,' M said. She learned, too, that Minnie had given her a name in the three short weeks she had her. Unlike many babies born 'without benefit of clergy', she said, she was able to keep that name forever.

M's original birth certificate confirmed that her surname

was Sinnett. Her records showed that she was fostered out from a Catholic orphanage when she was about two years old. She had no recollection of the place, but it is almost certainly St Joseph's in Broadmeadows (where Minnie had been placed for a short time before being sent back to the Oakleigh Convent Reformatory). M had many stories to tell about her foster mother, who had formally adopted her when she was 14. She had taken on the surname of her adoptive family, but nothing would shake her determination never to give up the Christian names that Minnie had given her in the few weeks of their life together.

M had been searching for her mother for many years using a variety of resources, including VANISH, a network that helps members of the adoption community find and connect with lost family members. All her efforts had resulted in frustrating dead-ends, until Minnie's death certificate led her to her mother's other 'oldest daughter'. Just as Lorraine was stunned to learn about her mother's secret life, M was equally surprised to learn that she now had five siblings. My mind slips back to the Ballarat Orphanage 60 years earlier, where Minnie, known then as Marie Green, played alongside Joyce Sinnett unaware they were sisters and with the Coombes children not knowing they were cousins.

During M's search for her mother, a social worker with access to Minnie's childhood files had told her that Minnie had had a 'sad, sad childhood'. M was pleased to learn that her mother had turned her life around. She saw her five happy adult siblings as proof of that. There was no fairy-tale ending for Minnie and her baby girl, no meeting between mother and daughter who'd lived separate lives for 70 years. I want to imagine the texture and flow of conversation had they met, but I can't get past the first tearful embrace.

25

Blighty 1953

I have given an account of all of Permella's children. But what about Frances, her eldest child, and my mother? On the rare occasions I heard my mother talk about her own mother, her words were strangely dispassionate. I never heard her say a bad word about her; but I never heard her say a good word about her, either. Maybe they were once close as mother and daughter. If so, did they discuss their dismal relationships with men and the disintegration of their families? If they did, did they agree that in those early years Frances was duplicating Permella's pathway?

Was there a time when my mother, like her mother before her, believed she would never regain custody of her children? Our father had been a convicted alcoholic—and maybe worse (Golding 2005). But following his last stint in gaol in mid-1947, he astounded everyone with his sudden transformation into a total abstainer. When their relationship stabilised, Permella would have seen saw how tenaciously Frances and Al set about retrieving us from the Ballarat Orphanage. It is reassuring to learn belatedly from the records that they made numerous requests to get us out of the Welfare and home with them (Wardship records 66851 and 66852; Golding 2005).

It's depressing to learn how hard it was for them to succeed in that goal. Our father's police record was just one of the impediments. He'd served his time through the penal system, but the Welfare produced its own separate standards of punishment. It laid down its own law in 1948 when it wrote that it would have to be satisfied that our father 'had borne a decent reputation for a considerable time before favourable consideration was likely to be given to returning any of the children to his custody'. They didn't define 'a decent reputation' or 'a considerable time'.

In 1950, my parents reckoned that more than two years was 'a considerable time' and tried again. This time, instead of our father who usually did the writing, our mother wrote the letter of application. She told the Welfare that our father had started a blacksmithing business in Naracoorte, South Australia, and they had rented a five-roomed house and fitted it out with beds and bedding for the three boys. I treasure this letter. 'My house will stand up to any inspection at any time by anyone,' my mother wrote. 'We know they will be terribly disappointed if they are not allowed to come home.' She added, shrewdly, that we might be tempted to run away and come to them if this application were to be rejected again.

My parents must have been infuriated when their plea was rejected. The Welfare kept giving different reasons. This time, it was because our parents had not 'regularised their association'. Presumably the Welfare believed that if you weren't married you couldn't bear 'a decent reputation'. Our release 'would be contrary to the best interests of the children', they asserted. By then, Bill was 15, Bob was 13 and I was 12. The Welfare defined our 'best interests' without feeling any need to discuss it with us or giving us a say. I recall the Orphanage Superintendent telling me that my father would not be allowed to visit again if he upset me. Nobody asked me if I was upset—and, if I was, why. Custody was out of the question, but the Welfare went further and issued our father a stern warning.

> *Mr Golding has been warned that he is not to unsettle the boys in any way during his periodical visits and if he does so, the Department will seriously consider refusing him access to them altogether* (CSV Ward file 68479).

My parents told us repeatedly that they would get us out of the Orphanage. I regret to say that I stopped believing them—perhaps that's what upset me then. It certainly upsets me now, when I learned about their constant futile efforts to get us home.

In 1951, my parents adopted another strategy. They rented a residence attached to a plumber's shop at 18 Main Road, Ballarat. This was only a short walk from the Orphanage hostel where Bob was living because he was by then put out to work. They could visit Bob more often, and this annoyed the superintendent, Eric Morton, who complained to the Welfare.

The Welfare had constructed a view of Frances and Al Golding as bad parents, and nothing would change that view. It exerted complete power and control over our family. But there was one simple thing they couldn't control: they couldn't stop us growing older. Bill and Bob had both left school and were sent to outside work—at the earliest legally approved age. Bill was being exploited as an unpaid labourer on a grazing property in western Victoria, while Bob was apprenticed—against his wishes—as a fitter and turner in Ballarat. I was attending the Ballarat High School—a rare chance that normally wasn't offered to Orphanage kids. The question of any future education had been raised although it was never discussed with me. I'm sure my parents never saw this internal memorandum.

> *Undoubtedly, all the boys will return to the mother and Golding in due course and it is just a question of whether he should*

be retained and given an education at the expense of the State when his future earnings will probably be collected by the mother (CWD File 66851).

This perverse memo expressed the commonplace ideology about tainted children and their unworthy parents that had been around for decades. A Royal Commissioner in 1878 advised what should be done with 12-year-olds who had been sent to school while in the 'care' of the state:

> *Let me first say, that under no circumstances ought they … be given back, as they sometimes now are, to the parents or relatives who have quietly looked on while the State was supporting them, until these have defrayed the whole charges of State maintenance. It is intolerable that, as sometimes happens, a man able to support his child should hand it over to the State because it is refractory, or because he finds that he can spend his wages more pleasantly than in feeding and clothing it, and should yet be allowed to intercept the profits of the child's labour when it becomes self-supporting* (Victoria 1878: 159).

In any event, in our case, Welfare ideology was finally undermined by the trilogy of happenstance, a sporting hero, and the Queen of England. In 1953, Walter Lindrum, the world champion billiards player, heard of a scheme to send 52 Australian boys to represent their municipalities at the coronation of Queen Elizabeth and to tour England and Scotland. Lindrum wanted an 'orphan' to have the same opportunity as these other boys. He organised a sportsmen's night and quickly raised the required sum of money for a scholarship. All orphanages in Victoria were asked to nominate candidates to sit an external exam. When the results came through, the Superintendent drove me and two other short-listed boys to the headquarters of Melbourne's biggest newspaper, the *Sun News-Pictorial*, which, together with the

Adelaide *Advertiser* and the Hobart *Mercury*, sponsored the travel scheme. In the boardroom, three men in dark suits interviewed a number of boys. After a nervous fortnight, I was told I was the lucky one. I don't know how my parents were told the news. Perhaps they read it in the papers.

Yet, I nearly didn't make it to England. Decades later, I discovered in the archives that Welfare headquarters had become agitated. An official advised his superiors that if I went on the overseas tour, I would miss a year's schooling and be nearly 17 before I got my Intermediate Certificate. He warned the Orphanage superintendent that he 'did not think that the Dept would be prepared to maintain the ward for that length of time & it was extremely unlikely that the father would do so even if he promised to do so'. The bureaucrat's arithmetic was poor. I missed just a term of school, not a year, and I was still just 15 when I passed all my exams and gained my Intermediate Certificate at the end of that year. Superintendent Morton reassured the Department that costs were not a problem. 'The father has agreed to provide the extra finance required in outfitting the lad for the trip. He has also assured me that if it were necessary to re-admit the lad to our Institution on his return from England he would certainly pay the cost of the boy's maintenance each week.'

I noted the words, 'if it were necessary to re-admit the lad to our Institution on his return from England'. They reveal that my travelling scholarship had created an unanticipated problem—more important than missing schooling or penny-pinching. The Head of the Welfare put his finger on the legal problem. Refusing approval for me to travel overseas would have been politically awkward after all the publicity published in *The Sun*, and echoed in the local media, the Ballarat *Courier* and radio 3BA. But there was more to it than that. A win for the boy would be a win for the parents—or at least give them an advantage in their ceaseless quest for reuniting their family. The Secretary of the Department summed up the problem:

> *As the boy is a ward of the Department, it will be necessary for me to obtain Ministerial approval for his departure from the jurisdiction form the State. I have no doubt that this will be forthcoming, but it might be a matter for consideration as to whether it might not be preferable to discharge him as a ward of the Department prior to his departure. I realize that such action would put the parents in an advantageous position should they seek custody on the boy's return, and even if they permitted him to remain with you for further schooling, you might find difficulty in securing regular voluntary payments from the father of the boy's maintenance. On the other hand, if the boy is to remain a ward, there is no guarantee, in view of his age, that the Department could continue boarding-out payments beyond the end of this year. Your comments on this aspect of the case will be appreciated.*

While Orphanage Superintendent Morton conceded that my parents would gain an (implied undeserved) advantage in seeking custody, he actually went further to support a proposal to discharge me from wardship. If I were no longer a state ward it would obviate the necessity of obtaining Ministerial approval for me to travel. Morton clinched the argument with a hitherto unheard word of praise for my father:

> *… I feel that by then the parents will be in a financial position to care for his future welfare. The father is certainly endeavouring to live a respectable life and at present is in good employment at Ballarat with Lewis Construction Company.*

Two days later, the Head sent a succinct note to the Orphanage: 'I desire to advise that I have decided to recommend to the Governor in Council that [Frank Golding] be discharged from the control of this Department.' After all the years of struggle, pain, and procrastination, the decision was made in the end with a quick stroke of a pen. Even a good word for my father. No one thought to tell me this stunning news at the time.

While I was sailing to England, the authorities realised their decision to discharge me had another consequence. What about my older brothers?

By the time my discharge was official, Bill had turned 18, and his wardship term had expired. Bob was now 16, and it would have appeared churlish not to set him free, too. Superintendent Morton acknowledged the difficulty of not acting:

> *Robert has been told by his father that on Frank's return from England he is going to have them both discharged from the Department, and this knowledge has had a definite retarded action on his behaviour at the Hostel. I would therefore recommend that Robert be permitted to return to his parents custody as soon as it is convenient.*

The Department responded:

> *It would appear that this boy's F/-[father] is now in regular employment & that he is trying to live down his past. (See File 66852 attached.) There seems to be no reason why Robert should not be discharged.*

Grandma Sinnett would have been astounded to learn that it was possible after all for parents to reclaim their lost children—even if it took more than a decade.

I knew none of this astonishing back-story of my release until I gained access to archived personal records when I was in my mid-50s. As an innocent 15-year-old steaming to

Blighty on the P&O liner, SS *Oronsay*, I had no inkling that I was carrying my passport to freedom. At the time, I thought my temporary relief would end after four months, so I had to savour every moment. From life as an institutionalised child where my every minute was regulated by electric sirens—get up, wash, eat, work, school, work again, eat again, play, wash, bed, lights out—I had such independence in London. Riding the Underground, catching the bright red double-deckers, treading many of the same streets my grandfather, Bill Sinnett, had trod in 1916 and 1917. We both had official passes. I read my grandfather's leave pass:

> *This pass may be withdrawn if the holder of it is unsteady or unsoldierly in conduct in any public place; if he is slovenly or untidy in appearance; neglects any soldier duty; does not salute properly; or breaks sanitary regulations against spitting on paths or roads or in public conveyances. The soldier on leave is expected to do credit to his uniform and to the Corps to which he belongs.*

And compare it with my Code of Conduct:

> *From now until next you tread Australian soil, your conduct is not a personal thing. You will be accepted as a typical Australian youth wherever you may go and all Australians will be judged on your own behaviour. This Code of Conduct, then, is given that you may do credit to your fair land and people. It is given also that you may avoid unnecessary dangers to your health and happiness which, if provoked by wilful or thoughtless act, could mar all the wonderful experiences that are ahead.*

My homecoming was dramatically different from my grandfather's. In 1919, he disembarked from the troopship *Tras os Montes*, and was met by a contrite and fearful wife expecting the worst. In 1953, disembarking from P&O's *SS Strathnaver*, I was met by my mother and father and the superintendent of the Orphanage. After a brief conversation about my new legal status, I was told it was my choice—back to the Orphanage or ... It took me a nano-second.

I had taken the long way home to family, and after 4 379 days as a child in the 'care' of the state, I was an orphan of the living no more. And my parents could be parents again.

The contrast between being confined in the Orphanage in April and being free to walk the streets of London in June 1953 was just the first of the transformations in my life. For years I was one among 200 inmates contending for personal space. Then suddenly I was a teenager in a family of five. I had slept in large, cold dormitories holding scores of children for more than a decade. Now all those long nights later, my mother tucked me into bed. Sweet dreams, deep safe sleep. The fear of nasties in the night now vanished. The rush of 200 children eating in silence exchanged for chatting at meals with just five at the table. Having laboured in jobs rostered for boys only, I was faintly embarrassed to be putting out the washing, and pegging out my mother's underwear. And doing the ironing and shopping. I'd never seen an adult sit and read a book. Never seen a father shaving. Never seen a mother putting on lipstick. Never seen dentures in a glass. Never had my own keys to the house. If you've spent the best years of your childhood in large institutions you have so much to learn. And as much to unlearn.

Our recovery as a family came with a question mark. Did it come too late? It was hard to know how to be a child in our family after all those years. It wasn't easy getting to know my mother and my father. They had lost many years too. It must have been hard for them as recovering parents. Biological likenesses aside, we were almost like strangers.

Resentment for the lost years was never more than an embarrassing moment away. A cup of tea and a biscuit might signal the start of a good chinwag in many families, but when my mother put the kettle on it was often a diversion from awkward questions.

'Who was Minnie?'

'I'll make us a pot of tea.'

'And Joyce?'

'Pass the sugar, Frankie.'

'What was it like to see your father for the first time when you were only three years old?'

'Run down to the shop to get me a packet of Havelock ready rubbed, would you Frankie?'

Yet, all the discomfort aside, I owe my parents a great deal. I was gratified to find many years later that my parents repeatedly implored the authorities to return their three boys. They were no match for the Welfare, but they never gave up. The Welfare thought 'those people' would exploit my education for their own selfish ends. They couldn't have been more off the mark. My parents insisted that I stay at school for as long as I was capable, for my own sake. On more than one occasion, one or other of them told me, 'You don't want to finish up like us.' They had both left school as soon as they were old enough to get a job—Dad even earlier, if I'm to believe his stories about chronic truancy from the age of eight. They knew their lack of qualifications locked them into a life of poorly paid and unfulfilling jobs. I knew they were intelligent and capable people. My mother could do the crossword quicker than most and managed Dad's blacksmithing invoices and handled his tax without mistakes. Dad knew exactly which horses were going to give trouble, and how to beat a lump of glowing steel into a tight-fitting shoe.

Their unwavering support, plus a system of bursaries and scholarships, plus hard work was the formula that saw me through high school, then to teachers' college, and eventually, to the Shop—our name for the Melbourne University. Unlike the box of grapes our father sent to us while we were in the Orphanage, the gift of education could never be taken away from me.

Coincidences sometimes seem unfathomable—but unexpected connections and continuities in history are not always cryptic. Years ago, Federation University Australia acquired the old Ballarat Gaol and converted it for educational purposes. I share a postgraduate research office there. In that very building Samuel Sinnett, my great uncle, was incarcerated as a young man. It's the same gaol that held Stanley Robinson, my mother's husband, and Al Golding, my father. Her stepfather, Jack Marone, died inside. My father would have said I've come up in the world. My office is not one of the old cells, but part of the Governor's quarters.

When the primary school inside the Ballarat Orphanage was opened it was blessed by a foundation stone appropriated from the wall of the Ballarat Gaol. When the Minister for Education, Mr Hutchinson, laid the foundation stone, his catchcry had been, 'Education is the best policeman' (*Argus* 28/7/1919: 4). The Minister's meaning may have been lost on the pupils of that school—including Joyce and Minnie Sinnett, my mother's sisters, her five Coombes cousins, and her first husband, Stanley Robinson and her children, Bill, Bob and me.

I was learning to read in that school in the 1940s at a time when Australia was helping to draft the Universal

Declaration of Human Rights which affirmed the family as "the natural and fundamental group unit of society … entitled to protection by society and the State" (Article 16.3). The ink soon dried on Australia's signature to the Universal Declaration, while my brothers and I languished in the emotional wasteland of a state-funded institution. Our family was 'entitled to protection', but the state ripped our family apart, shattered our lives, and created yet another generation of 'orphans of the living'.

26

Knowing better

When Edward Sinnett ran away from his brutish stepfather and stole a watch at 11 years of age in 1865, he would become the first of a long line of family members to grow up in what we now call out-of-home 'care' (OOHC). In this book, I have discussed only some of the more than thirty of Edward's descendants who, over five generations, were placed in a range of institutions for children or were fostered out or adopted. The vast majority of them had a living mother and father.

The welfare system itself was dysfunctional. It made decisions that caused harm to these fragmented families, not just to the children. Many of the children who were 'rescued' from poor families were no better off in the 'care' of the state or in the institutions run by churches and charities. Some were decidedly worse off as we now know from the testimony compiled in an accumulating number of formal inquiries.

Bureaucrats were at liberty to pass moral judgments and exercise control without accountability. People needed support; but vilification was easier, and it served to justify the way the Welfare treated so-called neglectful families. My parent's 'irregular domestic situation' was not a legal crime, nor was our illegitimacy, but to the Welfare it was justification enough to deny our return to our family.

It would be a mistake to conclude that the five-generational saga of the Sinnett family is unique. Multi-generational institutionalisation of children, we now know, is common (CLAN 2011; Royal Commission 2017: 154-155). Why does it happen? Some aspects of the Sinnett saga are characteristic of the OOHC system. Many survivors of an institutional childhood have reported they had serious problems in being parents when their biological turn came—often at a young age. Growing up without parents and sometimes separated from siblings, they suffered what an early Royal Commission called: 'the deadening influence of unexercised affection' (Victoria 1872: para. 10). They never saw a loving family in an intimate setting, never knew what was required to nurture their children, never saw how other parents nurtured and loved their children. Many survivors also report that they were so damaged in 'care' by the brutality and abuse—the utter betrayal of trust—that they never trusted anyone, let alone themselves, with their children. The existence of 'immoral practices of the worst kind' within institutions, was in plain sight of a colonial Royal Commission (Victoria 1872: para 48) in Edward Sinnett's time. Failure to take decisive action has resulted in a succession of damning inquiries that continue to 'discover' child abuse in institutions—reporting what many children in 'care' knew only too well, but were powerless to disclose.

Damaged children often become damaged adults. Some survivors have been so traumatised by their treatment as children and are so fearful of future abuse that they have chosen not to have children of their own. Evidence shows, however, that many young people who were raised in OOHC become parents at an early age, intentionally or not (Purtell et al. 2022). Those who do have children, and experience a crisis, avoid asking services for support because of anger at the way they were treated in the past and fear that authorities will use their 'record' as a warrant to interfere with their family—as was the case with Minnie Sinnett. Police and magistrates, child rescuers and social workers have been quick to pass judgment and condemn struggling families. They removed children from their family for protective reasons often masked in the ill-defined mantra of 'the best interests of the child'. Once scooped up by the Welfare, it was easy for a young person like Edward Sinnett to cross the fuzzy line from one status to the other, thereafter treated less for his needs and more for his deeds. Less protection and more correction.

This family saga shows it is facile to explain family dislocation simply in terms of the personal failings of parents, and therefore, responsible for their own plight. It is obvious that members of the Sinnett family had shortcomings, but that line of thinking hardly explains why my mother and her mother before her, and countless other mothers, made heart-breaking decisions about their children—or had them made by their betters. Behind every story of family disintegration is another story about people who, with little social support, found themselves trapped in long-term unemployment, unstable accommodation, and grinding poverty—all made worse by economic recession and war and the shadows of shame and self-blame.

The deep trauma of warfare and its aftermath of alcoholism, violence, mental illness, disillusionment, desertion and divorce brutally damaged the Sinnetts and their children. There were many families like them. In 1956, the superintendent of a Victorian reformatory for boys claimed that at least half the boys were 'war casualties…who had got out of control while their fathers were on service in World War II … [They were] boys who have been sharing the burden of the community thrust on them by the war.' (*Argus* 3/10/1956: 3). When we commemorate war, we should ask not just what our fathers and grandfathers did in war but what war did to them and to their families (Stephens 2014).

During the 2nd World War, the numbers of unmarried mothers increased, and many mothers were again 'compelled, by force of circumstances, to relinquish their rearing' (VPRS 4523/P/0001). The word 'relinquish' was tossed about airily, as if a mother could make a choice so simply. It wasn't abstract 'circumstances' that forced a mother like Permella Sinnett to give up her child. It was extreme pressure brought about by lack of support for a woman who was castigated as 'fallen'—in a completely different sense to the fallen soldier. A young woman who 'got herself into trouble' was 'ruined'. Framing the female as the problem allowed the state—and let's not forget the men involved—to be absolved of any moral duty to offer support.

Will there be a sixth generation of Sinnett children in OOHC? Over my dead body! I borrow those passionate words from another Care leaver who was adamant that no child of hers would suffer the same fate. Yet, we know that good intentions are not always enough to avoid repeating the worst of the past (CLAN 2011). There is no magic formula for breaking the cycle of multi-generational institutionalisation. The system itself is still deeply rooted in an ideology of patriarchy and punishment.

I can only speak for myself about how repeating history was avoided. Luck counted for a lot. The offer of an overseas trip when I was 15 changed everything for me and my family. 'Pure luck', I'm tempted to say. But the luck came at precisely the right moment in my parents' struggle for custody, and they seized the moment. My discharge generated opportunities that would not normally be open to state wards. Access to tertiary education was the most obvious benefit. Chance arrived with two reinforcements. The first was my parents' eagerness for me to continue at school for as long as I could, instructing me to do better in life than they did. The second was to have the wit to make the most of the scholarships that made access to education realistic for low-income families at that time.

Personal factors play a part too. At Teachers' College I once suffered a serious injury playing football and was confined to bed for a time. Two lecturers from the College paid a visit one day to ask how I was. I recall telling them I just had to get out of there. I knew my answer was ambiguous. I had developed an intense drive to move on to something better—and it wasn't just to get out of bed and back on the football field. In hindsight, I see it as a strong reaction to the many years of having no hope—not knowing when or if the bad times would end. I had become aware of a strength to bounce back from adversity, driven by hope and determination. Maybe, too, there has been an unconscious kicking back against those who believed orphanage children like me would never amount to much—the bigotry of low, or no, expectations (Harvey et al., 2015: 6).

Resilience is harder when you are socially isolated or have lost connection to family. Fragmentation of family can be irreparable. I never met any of my mother's sisters, except Catherine Marone—it is hard to refer to them as my aunts. Her mother was the only grandparent I met. My father had 16 siblings, but I can recall meeting only one of them. As if in compensation, I have been fortunate over the years to meet and connect with many good people who wanted the best for me. I was encouraged and stimulated by football coaches, school teachers, school inspectors, employers, colleagues, neighbours, just good friends, and ultimately a family of my own. I wish that all children who were once separated from their families were so fortunate.

Does a childhood of mistreatment and witnessing adults being hurtful to children generate a deep-seated consciousness that things must be changed if the world is to be a more humane place? Is that what drives my personal history of involvement in community activism and advocacy? And does this personal history, in turn, contribute to such a strong repulsion of the idea of state interference in my family that it renders any future intrusion inconceivable? Over my dead body will there be a sixth generation of Sinnetts in OOHC.

My great hope when I started my research was that I would find the story of my grandfather, William Francis Salvador Sinnett. I wanted to discover what manner of man he was. His story remains unfinished. His father's funeral in Ballarat in 1929 marked his last recorded public appearance and, despite the most exhaustive search, I can't find his final resting place. Was he one of those old bushies who simply died alone, and, when found, carried nothing to identify him? The Victorian Death Index lists 321 'unknowns' between 1929 and 1985. Perhaps Bill Sinnett adopted an alias and lived another life. Aliases were common in our family as we have seen.

No matter what the end of his life story may be, my grandfather was not the man I wanted him to be. I found a man who once loved, but could no longer love. A man who had come to see the futility of war, but couldn't make peace at home. A man who said he would forgive, but could never bring himself to be so generous.

Now at the end of this quest, I've made other discoveries I did not anticipate. I unearthed a compelling story about my mother and her mother. Permella's war was not on the hills of Gallipoli or the trenches of the Western Front, but her battles were no less destructive than Bill Sinnett's. If his darkest moment was being buried alive at the Somme, hers was finding that she would never be forgiven for a flash of passion. For that, she lost everything—the man she loved, her children, and the hope of a life fulfilled. She sacrificed everything to give the love of her life 'chances galore'. But the evidence shows she that while she didn't surrender without a fight the odds were too much for her.

Discovering this astonishing saga put an end to my long-held assumption that the reluctance of my grandmother and my mother to talk about our past was their way of shielding themselves and us from our painful childhood as orphans of the living. It is more likely that they lived with unresolved anger, guilt, shame, and despair and felt demoralised by being utterly powerless in the face of a system that showed no concern for them as parents. I am reminded of the compelling words of another mother who, twenty years earlier, had her child taken from her:

> *Can you imagine the shame? How do you ever tell anyone they took your kids away? You don't. You just look at the pavement for the rest of your life—even though you did nothing wrong except to have no one to help when things got bad (Harries, 2008: 35).*

Writing this book made me do what I had never thought to do before: envisage my mother as a child. My mother was not yet born when her father went off to the so-called Great

War. She was three years old when he finally returned. Then he made her hang by the fingernails over a chasm of fear. Half crazed by the brutality of the trenches at Gallipoli and the Western Front, Bill Sinnett wreaked havoc on his family. As a small child, my mother was the miserable witness to the manic humiliation and destruction. Collateral damage of the war that brought no peace. I can find no relief for her from that unremitting, remorseless loss and grief. That child lost so many of her family who might have provided love and joy: her three sisters and a little brother, her father and eventually even her mother and her siblings from her mother's second marriage. Two of her sisters, five of her first cousins, her niece, her uncle, her grandfather, were all lost to the Welfare. When, in turn, she lost her own three children, she was unable to share her grief with us.

I've long abandoned blame. How do you explain when the pain beats so deep? I wish I had known sooner the little girl who grew into the sad woman who locked up these dark memories. I wish I had known better that woman who was once my mother.

Bibliography

Primary Sources

Trove online at: http://trove.nla.gov.au/newspaper/ was accessed at various dates for the following contemporary newspapers: Ballarat *Courier*, Ballarat *Star*, Bacchus March *Gazette*, Bendigo *Advertiser*, Colac *Herald*, Geelong *Advertiser and Intelligencer*, London *British Australasian*, London *Times*, Mt Alexander *Mail*, Melbourne *Advocate*, Melbourne *Age*, Melbourne *Argus*, Melbourne *Herald*, Melbourne *Sun News-Pictorial*, Sydney *Smith's Weekly*.

Adams, Permella (1926). Affidavit and related documents, Supreme Court of Victoria [2007] VCS 510).

Ancestral Detective Agency (1998). *Hatches matches dispatches: An index of over 31 000 names from baptismal, marriage, burial/death records of Ballarat and surrounding areas*, Wendouree, the Agency.

Annual Reports (various dates). Note: the various government departments dealing with out-of-home Care in Victoria changed names frequently over the decades. For convenience, I have usually referred simply to the Department. Annual Reports were published by the Government Printer, Melbourne.

Australian War Memorial:
Australian Imperial Forces Routine Daily Orders for the period 1915–16. Australian Army War Diaries AWM4 – First World War at: http://www.awm.gov.au/diaries/ww1/diary.asp?diary=82.

Ballarat Orphanage (now Cafs, Ballarat). *Annual Reports*, Admissions Registers, School Rolls, and other resources held in the Heritage Centre, Ballarat.

Ballarat Orphan Asylum (1866). *2nd Annual Report* Committee of Management, Ballarat.

Consolidated Index to Ballarat & District School Student Registers. Australiana Research Room, Ballarat Municipal Library.
Index to Victorian Goldfields Hospitals Admissions (1856-1922) (2003)

Genealogical Society of Victoria

National Archives of Australia (various dates). *First Australian Imperial Force Personnel Dossiers, 1914-1920, B2455,* (including files for all soldiers mentioned in this book) online at: http://www.naa.gov.au/collection/explore/defence/service-records/index.aspx.

Public Records Office Victoria (various dates). Personal and family records obtained under Freedom of Information and related legislation; various coroners' reports, open ward files, probate, and other historic documents as cited.
VPRS 14: Register of Assisted British Immigrants 1839-1871.
VPRS 24/P, Coronial Inquests: Edward John Sinnett (1855/543); Francis Edward Salvador Sinnett (1926/906); Permella Agnes Marone (1972/1539); Thomas Matheson (1280, 8/9/1932); John Marone (1955/38).
VPRS 290/PO, Ballarat East Petty Sessions registers 1890-1921, Unit 63 Item 224: 22; and Unit 69 Item 191: 171RS.
VPRS 4523/P/0001, Grants to Orphanages, Unit 142, File Number 1379, 1924-1944.
VPRS 4527: State Ward Register.
VPRS 11976: Victorian Naval Training Ship for Boys Register, 1865-1876.
Probate Alice Sinnett #365772 dated 31/7/1945.

Victoria (various dates). *Government Gazette,* Melbourne, Government Printer.

Victoria (various dates). *Historical Index of Victorian Births, Deaths and Marriages,* Department of Justice, Melbourne.

Victoria (various dates) *Year Book,* Melbourne, Government Printer.
Victoria Police Gazette (*VPG*) (1853-1980). Melbourne, Government Printer.

Reports of Public Inquiries

Royal Commission into Institutional Responses to Child Sexual Abuse (2017). *Final Report: Vol. 11 Historical residential institutions,* Sydney, The Commission.

Senate of Australia, Community Affairs References Committee (2004). *Forgotten Australians: a report on Australians who experienced institutional or out-of-home care as children,* Canberra.

Senate of Australia, Community Affairs References Committee (2012). *Commonwealth Contribution to Forced Adoption Policies and Practices*, Canberra.

Senate Standing Committee on Social Welfare (1985). *Children in Institutional and Other Forms of Care: A national perspective*. Canberra, The Senate.

Victoria (1872). *Report no. 3 of the Royal Commission on Penal and Prison Discipline: Industrial and reformatory schools*, Melbourne, Government Printer.

Victoria (1878). *Public education: Royal Commission of Enquiry: Report on the state of public education in Victoria and suggestions as to the best means of improving it*, by Charles H. Pearson, Melbourne, Government Printer.

Victoria, Family and Community Development Committee (2013). *Betrayal of Trust: Inquiry into the handling of child abuse by religious and other non-government organisations*, Melbourne, PP No. 275.

Secondary Sources

Bean, C.E.W. (1921-1942). *The Official History of Australia in the War of 1914-1918. Volume I-X1: The Story of Anzac*, Sydney, Angus & Robertson.

Brogden, Joan (2000). *Neglected or Criminal? The Sunbury Industrial School: Vol. 3, Sunbury Reformatory: To the hulks and Jika*, Melbourne, Self-published.

Butler, A.G. (1940). *The Australian Army Medical Services in the War of 1914-1918. Vol. II: The Western Front*, Melbourne, Australian War Memorial.

Cannon, Michael (1996). *The Human Face of the Great Depression*, Mornington, self-published.

Care Leavers Australasia Network (CLAN) (2011). "Struggling to Keep It Together: A National Survey About Older Care Leavers Who

Were in Australia's Orphanages, Children's Homes, Foster Care and Other Institutions." Sydney, CLAN.

Carlyon, Les (2006). *The Great War*, Macmillan, Sydney.

Clendinnen, Inga (2006). The History Question: Who owns the past? *Quarterly Essay* 23.

Cossins, Annie (2013). *The Baby Farmers: A chilling tale of missing babies, shameful secrets and murder in 19th century Australia*, Sydney, Allen & Unwin.

Dennis, Peter et al. (1995). *The Oxford Companion to Australian Military History*, Melbourne, Oxford University Press.

Duke, M., Lazarus, A., & Fivush, R. (2008). Knowledge of family history as a clinically useful index of psychological well-being and prognosis: A brief report. *Psychotherapy Theory, Research, Practice, Training*, 45, 268-272.

Fraser, Don (2001). *Working for the Dole: Commonwealth relief during the Great Depression*, Canberra, National Archives of Australia.

Gamage, Bill (1975). *The Broken Years: Australian soldiers in the Great War*, Ringwood, Penguin Books.

Elena Georgiou (2005). Spoken and unspoken words in the life of a Cypriot woman in Thompson, Paul & Bertaux, Daniel (eds) *Between Generations: Family models, myths and memories*, London, Routledge.

Golding, Frank (2005). *An Orphan's Escape: Memories of a lost childhood*, Melbourne, Lothian.

Gorman, (Capt) Eugene (1919). *With the Twenty Second: A history of the 22nd Battalion AIF*. HH Champion, Melbourne, Revised Edition compiled by Carl Johnson, ed. by Carl Johnson and Kristine Braddock, (2001) Melbourne, History House.

Graves, Robert (1929, rev. 1957). *Goodbye to All That*, London, Penguin Books.

Harper, J. (2007). Judgment re application to inspect court file

P Sinnett v W Sinnett Proceeding No. 3 of 1926 [2007] VSC 510.

Harries, M. (2008). The Experiences of Parents and Families of Children and Young People in Care: A social research project undertaken by Anglicare WA, on behalf of Family Inclusion Network W.A.

Harvey, A., McNamara, P., Andrewartha, L. & Luckman, M. (2015). Out of Care, into University: Raising higher education access and achievement of care leavers, Bundoora, LaTrobe University.

Howe, Renate & Swain, Shurlee (1993). *The Challenge of the City: The centenary history of Wesley Central Mission 1893–1993*, Melbourne, Hyland House.

James, Margaret (1979). `Double Standards in Divorce: Victoria, 1890 – 1960', in *In Pursuit of Justice: Australian women and the law 1788 – 1979*, eds. J. Mackinolty and H. Radi, Sydney, Hale & Iremonger.

McKernan, Michael (1980). *The Australian People and the Great War*. Sydney, Collins.

Miller, Geoffrey (1993). 'The Battle of 3rd Ypres (Passchendaele)', Text of a talk at: http://net.lib.byu.edu/estu/wwi/comment/ypres3.html (viewed 26/3/2010.)

Musgrove, Nell (2024 in press). Emotion as a Tool for Humanising Histories of the Marginalised: A Case Study of Industrial Schools in Colonial Victoria. *Social History*, 44(1).

Purtell, J., Mendes, P., Saunders, B., & Baidawi S., (2022). Healing Trauma and Loss and Increasing Social Connections: Transitions from Care and Early Parenting, *Child & Adolescent Social Work J*ournal, 39, 735–747.

Qartly, Marian, Swain, Shurlee & Cuthbert, Denise (2013). *The Market in Babies: Stories of Australian adoption*, Melbourne, Monash University Publishing.

Robson, L.L. (1970). *The First AIF: A study of its recruitment*, Melbourne, Melbourne University Press.

Scott, Ernest (1936). *The Official History of Australia in the War of 1914-1918, Vol. XI: Australia During the War*, Sydney, Angus and Robertson.

Spearitt, Katie (1988). *The Poverty of Protection: Women and marriage in colonial Queensland 1870-1900*, Honours thesis, University of Queensland.

Stanley, Peter (2010). *Bad Characters: Sex, crime, mutiny, murder and the Australian Imperial Force*, Sydney, Pier 9.

Stanley, Peter (2011). *Digger Smith and Australia's Great War: Ordinary name, extraordinary stories*, Sydney, Pier 9.

Stephens, David (2014). 'Tangled up in red, white and blue', *Honest History*, at: http://honesthistory.net.au/wp/red-white-and-blue/ (viewed 21/5/2014.)

Swain, Shurlee (2012). 'Snapshots from the Long History of Adoption in Australia', *Australian Journal of Adoption*, Vol. 6, No. 1.

Warhaft, Sally (ed.) (2004). *Well May We Say: The speeches that made Australia*, Melbourne, Black Inc.

Acknowledgments

In researching this book, I discovered previously unknown members of my extended family. They shared family lore and provided genealogical leads and rare family photographs. Thank you, Leanne, Lynette, Deborah, Peter, Eve-Lynne and two Lorraines.

I value the work of communities of academics who understand the value of insider knowledge in contributing to research into policy in child and family welfare. My thanks to David McGinniss and Jacqueline Wilson, colleagues at Federation University Australia, Joanne Evans and Sue McKemmish at Monash University, Shurlee Swain and Nell Musgrove at the Australian Catholic University, and Cathy Humphreys at the University of Melbourne.

Staff at Find & Connect, especially Cate O'Neill, offered generous support. I commend the excellent web resource: http://www.findandconnect.gov.au. I thank the Public Records Office of Victoria, National Archives of Australia, Australian War Memorial and Ballarat Cafs for making personal records more accessible than they once were.

I learned a lot from regular workshopping at Writers Victoria especially with Debi Hamilton, David Francis and Hannah Robert. I am also indebted to two of Victoria's best writers and teachers of writing, Josieane Behmoiras and Maria Tumarkin for advice and encouragement.

Closer to home, Major Daryl Hockings (ret) C.S.M. willingly fielded my queries about military matters. I miss you, Daryl. Heather Hockings read a draft manuscript with care, but also, her wicked humour ensured her 'neighble' didn't get too full of himself. I miss you, too, Heather.

I am proud to be a Life Member of Care Leavers Australasia Network (CLAN). This peak organisation provides fearless advocacy and support for many of the hundreds of thousands of Australians who grew up in orphanages, children's Homes, youth detention centres, reformatories, industrial schools and in foster care. I admire the courage and tenacity of Clannies everywhere, and Leonie Sheedy OAM in particular. We never give up in the search for justice! (Contact: 1800 008 774; www.clan.org.au).

Writing about fragmented families over generations has made me ever more appreciative of my amazing children—Lindy, Peter, Tim and Dan—and their own wonderful partners—Michael, Alex, Nick, and Emily—and their children, James, Sam, Eleanor and Tom, my grandchildren. I love them all dearly. I'm so lucky to live with Lizzie Moore Golding, a perceptive reader, a great artist, and a loving partner.

Index

www.ingramcontent.com/pod-product-compliance
Ingram Content Group UK Ltd.
Pitfield, Milton Keynes, MK11 3LW, UK
UKHW041636190726
13854UKWH00006B/2516

9 781923 068759